GOTHIC
GHOST
STORIES

A.S. Mott

Ghost House Books

To all the girls in black dresses and
white makeup whom no one understands

Stay Goth

Contents

Acknowledgments

I would like to thank my editor, the incomparable Shelagh Kubish, for once again taking a criminally haphazard collection of sentences and paragraphs and turning it into the tidy, literate package you hold in your hands. I would also like to thank Lee Craig, who aided Shelagh in her duties and in doing so suffered just as much.

Thanks must also be given to Jessica Dean, the artist responsible for this book's drawings, as well as to Jeff Fedorkiw and Gerry Dotto who combined everything together and turned the stories and drawings into the type of thing that actually deserves to be sold in stores.

And finally, I must thank Nancy Foulds and Shane Kennedy for letting me have some fun on a project I really enjoyed putting together.

Introduction

I ACTUALLY PUT THE DEFINITION OFF UNTIL I was just two weeks from finishing this book. Even before I started writing it, people had been asking me—whenever the discussion turned towards my latest project—what a "gothic" ghost story is and how it is any different from a regular ghost story. I found this question hard to answer. I mean, I know exactly what Gothicism is and can name countless examples of the style, but describing it has proven as difficult as giving an accurate description of the feeling of melancholy. Sad and gray and regretful give you a sense of the emotion, but in the end, these words prove entirely inadequate. It was because of this lack of a concrete definition that I kept reminding myself to look up the word "gothic" in the paperback dictionary I keep within arm's reach of my computer's keyboard. But, because procrastination is the watchword of any true writer, I kept putting this off, until the book was nearly finished and I had already decided what my personal definition of Gothicism is.

It's a good thing I didn't look it up right away, because I don't know what I would have done if I had looked up the term when I started, because this is what I found:

Gothic *adj.* **1:** of or relating to the Goths **2:** of or relating to the style of architecture prevalent in Western Europe from the middle 12th century to the early 16th century

Who then are the Goths? Well, according to the same dictionary, they were a "Germanic race that early in the

Christian era overran the Roman Empire." But we all know that isn't completely true. Chances are, if you're anything like me, you've known plenty of Goths in your lifetime and even if they did happen to be German, they were far too busy listening to The Cure to overrun a pizza place, much less the entire Roman Empire. So, while the dictionary definition of the word gothic is literally true, it is, in the end, as inadequate as my attempt to describe the feeling of melancholy. Today it is very easy to be a modern Goth and know nothing about the history of European Gothic architecture or of the invaders who finally took down the imperial Romans. For many, all it takes is a preference for dark clothing, pale skin and a taste for the macabre. But even this formula doesn't amount to the whole truth.

So what is that truth? Well, to paraphrase a quotation I first heard from the author and television host Daniel Richler, Gothicism at its heart "is when sex and death get together on the dance floor."

Fear is the natural human reaction to anything that can harm us. It is the warning signal our brains emit whenever we put our mortality into jeopardy. Whenever we are afraid, the reason for that fear, regardless of the cause, is that we think we are going to die. And what Gothicism does is take that fear of death and turn it into something desirable. Instead of being repulsed by that which may kill us, we are attracted to it. Regardless of the setting or the clothing or the characters (although those are all important elements), the difference between a gothic ghost story and a regular ghost story is that in a gothic ghost story you want to love that which you should be afraid of. In a gothic ghost story beauty is not something you should embrace, but something you should avoid.

All of the following six stories deal somehow with the notion of the complications of beauty. Some of the stories are dark and bleak in their assessment of human nature, while others are more optimistic in their outlook.

The book begins with "The Last of the Seven Brothers," which came about as a result of my attempts to describe my vision of Gothicism to others. Inevitably, I found myself describing the famous fairy tale "Snow White and the Seven Dwarfs," which—with its pale heroine and a plot obsessed with death and beauty—struck me as the one truly gothic story that everyone can relate to in some fashion. It then occurred to me that because this was the case, it made perfect sense to continue the story and take it to the next level. I had no idea when I started it just how long it would take me to get there.

The second story, "Business As Usual," is likely to cause some controversy, as it is set inside an office building, which is not normally considered an apt setting for a gothic tale. What the most literal readers might forget is that the story is firmly set in the world of Film Noir, a style that originated in '40s gangster and detective films and that can easily be described as modern urban Gothicism. With its shady cast of characters, including the overly ambitious protagonist, the gorgeous femme fatale and the unlikable patsy who yearns for revenge, this story is probably the darkest to appear between these pages.

In "The Girl in the Water" I have taken the most famous gothic ghost story of all time (although I suspect few of you have ever heard it described that way) and retold it from the point of view of a character who often gets ignored in most renditions of the tale. When I finished it I was surprised to discover how much power and control over the situation this character actually possessed and how her traditional portrayal as a helpless pawn in a game she cannot control is only a very narrow interpretation of who she really is. I especially like the fact that, whether you agree with what she does or not, she turns out to be a far stronger person than the tragic hero the story usually celebrates. She can do what he can only soliloquize about.

"Only Pretend," the fourth story, is my tribute to the great horror films produced by Hammer Films, the now-defunct British production company. For three decades, from the 1950s to the 1970s, they produced a series of films that defined for many the true gothic style. Often formulaic and cheaply produced, these films still manage to stand the test of time thanks to their devotion to period settings, deep red blood, horrible monsters and beautiful woman in impressively cleavage-baring outfits.

Based on a story I first wrote about in my book *Ghost Stories of America II,* "Empathy" is a gothic tale about a young Confederate wife who risks everything to save her captured husband. The moral of this story is that sometimes those who do wrong to others do so not out of evil, but instead because they have no other choice.

And, finally, the last story in the book is titled simply "The Goth Girl." It, like this whole book, is dedicated to the young women I grew up with who rebelled against the status quo and who chose to follow their own style, even at the risk of social alienation. For reasons of plot, many of the women in this book are described as being "the most beautiful" woman the other characters have ever seen, but in my mind the title character in this story is the one who truly deserves that designation. Of all the women I have written about in these pages, she is the only one I have ever met and maybe the only one who really exists at all.

—A.S. Mott

The Last of the Seven Brothers

IT WAS A COLD AUTUMN MORNING. The newly risen sun shone through Wexel's bedroom window and bathed his face with warm light, waking him like it always did. He stretched and yawned and slid out of his bed, shivering in the chilly air as he changed into his dirty work clothes. His body felt tired and sore as he stepped into his handmade coveralls and pulled on his heavy woolen sweater. He had worn these clothes every day for the past 10 years, and they were covered with patches from past splits and tears and with stains that simply refused to be cleaned away. He would have replaced them with new clothes years ago, but his brother Henson had been the one who had done all the sewing and he had been dead nine and a half years now. Wexel could have gone to the market to buy new pants and a sweater, but all they ever had in his size were clothes for young children that made him look foolish and laughable. The clothes Henson had made for all of them could easily have fit a child of six, but looked as though they belonged on a man at least three or four feet taller. He pulled a woolen cap over his small bald head and—ready for breakfast—cocked his ear towards his door, listening to the sounds of the house to hear if he was the first one up. Hearing only silence, he assumed he was.

He walked out of his small room and knocked on his brother's door.

"Gedrick," he said, "it's time to get up."

There was no response, but that wasn't unusual. Gedrick had always been a sleepy sort of fellow and he had grown even fonder of his bed as he had gotten older. Wexel let him sleep and went into the kitchen, certain that the smell of warm oatmeal would be enough to rouse his brother out of bed.

"Time to boil the water," he said aloud to no one. Over the past couple of years he had developed the habit of talking to himself, which was odd considering that when he was younger he had spoken so little that many had assumed he was mute. Back then there had been so many voices fighting to be heard that he—the youngest of them all—knew it was futile even to try to get a word in on the then-constant conversation. But now that the house was so eerily silent and his brothers' absence so obvious, he felt obligated to speak aloud whenever he could.

He boiled the water and poured it over the oats, and the warm smell wafted throughout the kitchen, warming his nose. He was hungry and ate quickly, waiting for Gedrick's door to open and for his yawning brother to stumble towards the kitchen table in search of nourishment. But Gedrick did not rise.

Worried, Wexel got up and knocked once again on his brother's door.

"It's time to go to work," he insisted. "You can't sleep forever."

There was only silence.

Wexel opened his brother's door, and his heart froze when he did not hear the gentle snores that were always present when Gedrick was asleep. He ran to his brother's bed and grabbed his hand. It was cold. It was very cold.

Wexel began to cry. Not just because his brother was dead, but also because—after a lifetime with his brothers—he was now alone.

A few minutes passed. He dried his tears and walked out of their small home in the forest and grabbed one of the small shovels that sat lined against the railing of the front porch. With it in his hand, he walked to the small clearing where his five other brothers were all buried, and he dug a new grave.

"I wonder," he asked himself, "who will do this for me when I am gone?"

It didn't take him long because he was a strong digger and the grave was small. When he was finished, he took the shovel back to the house and found a hammer, a saw, some nails and some spare wood. An hour later he had a small casket ready for his brother. He looked at it and felt guilty.

"The others were so much better," he said, criticizing himself. He had never been the best carpenter, and as a result, Gedrick would be getting a casket nowhere near as nice as those that had been crafted for the others. It was then that his memory drifted back to years and years ago, when he was just 16. He remembered the first time they had to build a casket. They had all been so heartbroken about the death of whom they were building it for that they had vowed to build the most beautiful one ever crafted. They built it out of glass and decorated it with diamonds and gold.

"That one had a happy ending," he said to himself as he walked into Gedrick's room and lifted his brother out of his bed. He carried him to the casket and placed him in it. He covered it and nailed it shut and wheeled it to the freshly dug grave. He lowered the casket in as best he could and said a short prayer before he covered it with dirt and went back to the house to chisel out a small gravestone. He finished it just as the morning ended and placed it at the foot of the grave. He said another prayer, and he cried some more.

Eventually he made his way back to the cabin, which was now as quiet and empty as it had ever been in his entire

lifetime. Sitting in the kitchen, he couldn't even hear the sounds of the forest outside. It was as if nature was mourning his loss as much as he was. He thought about going to the mine and getting half a day's worth of work done, but now the idea of work seemed so pointless. Over the years they had pulled so many riches out of their secret mine that they could have all comfortably stopped working 20 years ago, when Befler was the first to die, thanks to a powerful sneeze that caused the tunnel he was in to collapse. But they had kept working; it was all they knew how to do. The reality was they had no need of the fortune they had accumulated. They took what they needed from the forest and only very rarely went into the nearby villages for supplies. They had all hated the way strangers stopped and stared at them, whispering to each other as they passed. In the forest they were a family, but in a village they were nothing but a collection of freaks.

Needing to break the horrible silence, Wexel found his harmonica and put it to his lips and played a long sad tune. As he played, he wondered what he would do with the rest of his life. Without work and without his brothers, his life was now without purpose. Not knowing how long he had left to live, the thought of decades of loneliness and boredom was enough to make him put down his harmonica.

As he sat and pondered his seemingly desolate future, he remembered the one and only time someone outside of his family had been a part of his life. It had been 34 years since he had seen her last, that magical day when a simple kiss had transformed the finest casket ever made into a superfluous glass box. In his life he had seen very few women, but in his heart he knew that she must have been the most beautiful in the world. Her lips had been as red as blood. Her skin as white as snow. Her eyes as blue as an azure flood and her hair as dark as coal. From the first second he had seen her, huddled and frightened along a dark forest path, he had loved her. And though he never told her, he knew that she knew. She knew that they all loved her. The seven of them knew a true treasure when they found it, and they all basked in her presence for as long as fate allowed. But they all knew that she was a treasure they did not deserve and when it came time to give her up, they did so without a word or regret.

Wexel allowed himself to smile for the first time that day as he recalled the kiss she had given him on his forehead just before she had left them. As soft and quick as that kiss had been it was the only one he had ever known, and the thought of it was enough to make him forget his troubles for a brief moment. His stomach rumbled and he looked out the kitchen window and was surprised to see the sunset. The day was ending, and it felt like it had just started.

He got up, lit some candles and started making a stew for his supper. He was nearly finished when he realized he had made enough for two. He would have to remember to half all his recipes. But, because he had not eaten since breakfast, he was hungry enough to eat all of it. He could feel the silence around him as he ate. At least now the forest had come back to life, and he heard the wind and the trees and the animals outside. He looked out the window again and saw storm clouds brewing in the sky. Rain began to fall, soon followed by equal measures of thunder and lightning.

Full of stew, he suddenly became very sleepy and quickly cleaned up his mess in the kitchen before he decided to go to bed. The storm had caused the house to turn very dark, and he made his way to his room guided by a single candle. The tumult outside didn't frighten him; his brother Henson had always been the bashful one in the family, but he did feel uneasy about sleeping in an empty house. He couldn't think of anything that could go wrong, but just the newness of the experience was enough to make him anxious.

He got to his room and quickly changed into his nightshirt. He climbed onto his bed and covered himself with his thick, warm blankets and blew out the candle, plunging the room into a heavy darkness that was alleviated only by the occasional flash of lightning outside. He closed his eyes and waited for sleep to come. It took a lot longer than it usually did, but eventually, after a couple of hours, he faded into his dreams.

In them he found himself in a very dark place. It was cold and damp, but somewhere—high above his head—was a flicker of light. There was someone with him, but it was too dark to see who it was. Whoever it was smelled very bad and unnerved him with constant whispering. Though he could barely hear it, the voice sounded as though it was coming from an old woman. He had to strain his ears to hear what she was saying, but eventually he was able to figure it out.

"A little light and a little time is all I need," the woman whispered, "to make right her wretched crime, her heinous deed."

He didn't know what this was supposed to mean, but the woman kept repeating it. She never once stopped, until, finally, after what seemed like years in the darkness, the light high above their heads grew and grew. In his dream he had to shield his eyes for fear of being blinded by it, it became so bright. He could now see that they had been buried deep beneath a pile of rocks, and the light was the result of their being lifted away. He turned and saw the face of the woman he had been trapped with. He began to shake when he saw it. He had seen her before. It had been so long ago, but hers was a face he could never have forgotten. It was an old face, too old to be human. Wrinkled and rotten, her skin was also mottled and gray and covered with warts and long black hairs. Her teeth were black and cataracts blinded her eyes, but this did not matter because she did not need her eyes to see. As the rocks were moved away, she quit whispering and started to laugh. It was a dry, painful cackle that hurt his ears to hear it.

"Mirror calls and mirror wakes," she shouted to the world, "and fairness falls and ravage takes!"

Wexel could do nothing but watch as this decaying bag of bones crawled out from the rubble and killed the two men who had been moving the rocks. It took her only a few seconds and with all the effort of swatting a pair of pesky mosquitoes. As old and frail as she looked, she was possessed by a power that was not human and made her stronger than any man.

Before he could climb out of the hole, she was out of sight, but he heard her horrible laugh as it echoed in the forest. He closed his eyes and when he opened them again his dream had taken him somewhere new. He had never seen this place before, but it appeared to be what his imagination had always assumed the inside of a castle looked like. There, in the corner, he saw a woman asleep on a small bed. He recognized her instantly. He was stunned by how little she had changed since he had seen her last. She was 30 years older, but she still looked like a young girl.

"Giselle," he whispered to her, but she did not hear him.

He started to approach her, but before he got to her, the door to her room burst open. He turned and saw the dried decaying figure of the old woman.

"Mirror calls and mirror wakes," she hissed at them, "and fairness falls and ravage takes!"

The witch lunged forward towards Giselle, and—on instinct—he threw himself between them, but the old crone passed through him as though he wasn't even there. He watched helplessly as the monstrous hag grabbed the woman he had once loved and lifted up the claw-like fingers of her withered right hand and plunged them deeply into Giselle's chest. Giselle woke and screamed until the pain was enough to kill her, and the witch pulled out her warm red heart.

Wexel began to scream. He screamed so loudly he woke himself and fought against the heavy weight of the blankets on top of him. He fell out of his bed and began to hyperventilate as he shook on the floor. The air was cold, but his skin was covered with sweat. Tears poured out of his eyes, and he cried for several minutes before he was able to remember that it had just been a dream.

"But I've never had a dream like that," he reminded himself. It was true. In all of his life he had never had a dream that had felt so real. Even though he knew it was crazy, a part of him felt as though the dream had been a warning. He did not believe in omens or prophecies, but he was old enough now to know that a lot of things he did not believe in might be true. And if the dream was a warning, then that meant the only woman he had ever loved was in danger. If that was true, he could not live knowing he had done nothing to try and save her.

As he dressed, the storm continued outside. It would be several hours until the sun rose, but he could not wait. He found an old leather bag and packed it with some food, water, gold nuggets and other supplies. He left the cabin and grabbed a pickax that had been leaning against the porch. The wind was cold and rough and the rain felt sharp against his skin, but he was too determined to notice his own discomfort. There was one place where he could find out for certain if what he had dreamt was really going to happen, and it would take him a few hours to get there.

• • •

The storm had finally ended just as he began to approach the edge of the cliff at the end of the southern forest. For him and his brothers, the cliff had always been the symbolic marker of the beginning of the unknown world. It was as far as any of them had ever traveled north, and the little they knew about what lay beyond it came only from rumors and stories they had heard in the nearby southern villages. According to this hearsay, the north was a land of rogues, scoundrels and thieves, where honest men were murdered purely for sport. Worse, it was said to be a land heavily populated by practitioners of the black arts, who honed their dark skills by cursing anyone unlucky enough to pass them on their way.

Wexel tried not to think of these stories as he tied a length of strong rope to a tree at the cliff's edge and lowered it to the ground below. The cliff was not very high, only a couple of 100 feet, but to a dwarf who got uncomfortable standing on a step stool, it was an unimaginable distance. He closed his eyes and very slowly climbed down the rope to the ground below.

When his feet finally touched the ground, he opened his eyes and nearly wept with relief. The sunrise was still a few minutes away, but the first hints of dawn were enough to allow him to spot a vague shape in the distance. He slowly

made his way towards it, but he tripped over something before he was halfway there. He got up and looked down to see what he had tripped on. It was a normal-sized pickax. The kind a man would use if he was digging out a pile of rocks. Wexel's heart began to race, and he ran towards the inert shape and found to his horror that it was the body of a middle-aged man. He checked for a pulse, but it was obvious that the man was dead. Wexel turned and saw the body of another man lying facedown on the ground just a few feet away. He began to shake as he slowly moved forward and found the hole they had been digging in the pile of rock, which had previously sat undisturbed for over 30 years.

Seeing it, his memory flashed back to that horrible night when he and his brothers had all vanquished the evil woman who had come to kill Giselle, by chasing her to the edge of the cliff. He remembered standing there, wondering what they were going to do next, when nature solved their problem by sending down a bolt of lightning that struck the ground at the woman's feet. The earth exploded, and she was thrown off the cliff and buried beneath a ton of heavy rock on the ground below. They had all assumed that she was gone forever. He now knew they had been wrong. She had just been waiting and now she was back.

The sun rose in the sky as he stood and tried to think of what he would do next. He had to warn Giselle before it was too late, but he didn't know where she was. She had been carried away from them by a prince, but from what kingdom the young man came he didn't know. Not knowing what else to do he got down on his knees and prayed to his brothers for guidance.

"There is so little time," he whispered, "tell me what to do."

It was then a voice spoke in his mind. He couldn't tell if it was his or someone else's, but it said: *Go north.*

That was all he needed. He stood back up, picked up his small pickax and leather bag from the ground and started walking north.

• • •

Even though the northern forest was just a forest and its trees were simply trees, Wexel could not stop feeling anxious and afraid as he moved through it. It seemed darker and less welcoming than what he was used to, and the animals he heard sounded larger and infinitely more menacing than those he had encountered before. He felt not a single moment of ease as he walked, his head turning at the slightest echo in the distance. He feared not only the animals, but also the possibility of running into thieves, murderers and sorcerers. Worse, he feared that he might come across the horrible creature that had driven him into this situation, the demonic hag who had risen from the ground after an uncomfortable three-decade nap. He knew that he would be no match for her and that if she found him, he would not live long enough to warn Giselle.

After five hours of walking, he sat down and rested and ate some of the food from his pack. He wondered what he would do when night came, unsure if he could ever relax enough in this strange forest to sleep. He stopped eating when he heard what sounded like a twig snapping in the distance. He heard it again. And again. Someone was walking nearby and heading his way.

"I have to hide," he whispered to himself as he frantically turned and looked for a place where he could disappear. For most men, there would have been few choices, but for a man of his size there were many. He chose the hollowed-out center of an old dead tree. As he stepped into it, he frightened a small squirrel, which ran away from him with an annoyed look. Like all people trying to hide, he became immediately aware of just how noisy he was when he wasn't making any noise at all. He held his breath and tried to calm his heart, fearing it was beating so loud it might give him away. The sound of the footsteps drew closer and closer. Whoever it was walked slowly and with confidence. They were in no hurry to get where they were going, but they had no doubt that they were going to get there. He exhaled as quietly as he could and took in another deep breath and waited for the stranger to pass by, but when the sound of the footsteps were at their loudest and it was clear the person was only a foot or so away from the old dead tree, they suddenly stopped.

The hollow tree echoed as a wooden walking stick banged against it.

"You needn't hide from me dwarf," said the stranger in an old and slightly bemused voice. "I know you're in there."

Wexel stayed quiet and did not move.

"I am very old and very patient, so I can wait far longer than you can," said the voice, "so please save us the bother and get out now. I swear I mean you no harm."

His heart racing and petrified that the voice belonged to a sorcerer capable of transforming him into some tiny insignificant animal, Wexel knew that there was nothing he could do and he slowly stepped out of the tree's hollow. The first thing he saw was a shriveled old man, whose back was hunched over with either age or truly horrible posture.

"There you go," the old man said with a smile, "nothing to fear."

Wexel held onto his pickax, ready to use it if he had to.

"How did you know I was there?" he asked the man.

"Loretta told me," the man answered him.

"Who's Loretta?"

The old man smiled again and turned and held out his hand. From beneath a fallen tree the squirrel Wexel had annoyed ran out and jumped into the man's outstretched palm.

"A squirrel told you where I was?"

The man nodded.

"A squirrel named Loretta?"

"That's right. She wasn't very happy about your invasion of her space. She has half a winter's collection of food stored in there and she feared you were going to take it from her."

"I'm sorry," Wexel apologized, before he realized he had failed to ask the obvious question. "You really can talk to squirrels?"

"It is a strange skill, I know," the old man admitted, "but it isn't the strangest I have picked up in my time here."

"I bet."

"I have never seen you around here before," said the man. "Am I to assume you come from the southern forest?"

"That's right," answered Wexel, loosening his grip on his pickax.

"I have never been to the southern part of the forest. I hear it is full of murderers, thieves and all manner of evil folk. Is this true?"

"No," Wexel said as he shook his head. "Where I come from they say the same things about the northern forest."

"I wonder then—if they are not here in the south or there in the north—where are all these foul criminals to be found?"

"The east or the west, maybe?" Wexel said and allowed himself to smile.

"Perhaps," nodded the old man, "perhaps."

The old man then gave Loretta a pat on her head and put her back down on the ground, where she ran to her tree and stared at Wexel suspiciously.

"Are you hungry?" asked the old man.

"I was eating just before I heard you coming near," Wexel answered him.

"Then I have disturbed your lunch. Come with me and I'll make up for it." The old man started to walk away.

Wexel started to protest, fearing he didn't have any time to waste, but then he remembered he still didn't know where he was going and that the old man might at least be able to answer some questions that would help him out. He followed him to a shack that stood in a clearing half a mile from the hollowed-out tree. As slowly as the old man walked, Wexel still had to struggle to keep up because three of his steps equaled one of the old man's.

The old man had a bowl of potato soup bubbling in a pot over the fire in his ramshackle hearth. He spooned out two bowls, and the two of them sat down at an old and splintery table to eat.

"I take it your reason for being so far away from home is very important to you, if you were willing to enter a forest you believed was so dangerous," said the old man after they were done eating.

Wexel nodded.

"I had a dream," he explained. "A nightmare."

"Ahhh," the old man smiled. "Someone is in danger."

"Yes."

"A lost love?"

Wexel paused before he answered this.

"A love, yes, but I never lost her. We let her go. It would not have been right to force her to stay."

"We?" asked the old man.

"Me and my brothers. There were seven of us." Wexel took a deep breath before he started to tell the tale. "Many years ago we came across this frightened girl in the forest. She had been left there by a minion of her stepmother's, a vile and wicked woman, who had ordered the minion to kill her and cut out her heart, but he could not do it and he ordered her to run away. She had been running for hours when she finally collapsed from exhaustion and we found her. We took her home and healed her cuts and wounds and let her rest for as long as she needed. She was so beautiful. We all fell in love with her. When she was better she returned the favor by taking care of us." Wexel smiled as he recalled the memory. "She wasn't very good at doing household chores, but she tried as hard as she could and we were too happy to have her around to complain or even notice. Then," his smile faded, "we came home from the mine one day and spotted an old woman leaving our cabin. Fearing the worst we ran to the house and found her lying dead on the kitchen floor, murdered by a poisoned piece of fruit. Enraged, we chased after the old woman. We ran for hours and it was only when we cornered her at the edge of a cliff that we came close to exacting our revenge, but none of us knew what to do. We were not violent men. Finally, a lightning bolt sent the foul witch over the edge of the cliff where she was—we thought—forever buried under a pile of rock.

"We went back to our cabin and decided to build our beloved girl the most beautiful casket ever devised. We crafted it from glass and lined it with the largest and finest gems we had ever unearthed. We placed her in it and mourned her passing. As we wept, a young man came riding from out of the forest. He wore the colors and the crest of a prince and he was taken aback by the sight of seven small men weeping over a girl in a glass box, but then he took a closer look at the girl and immediately understood. He got off his horse and asked us who she was. We told him and he asked us if he could give her a kiss. We thought it a strange thing to ask, but we said yes. He walked over to her and opened the casket and bent over and gave her a kiss on her lips."

Wexel's lip began to tremble as he recalled what happened next. "She was dead! That was never in doubt. She was dead! But there was magic in that kiss, a magic none of us even knew was possible. He kissed her and her eyes opened. She sat up and asked us why we all looked so sad. She was alive! The prince's kiss had brought her back to life! We cheered and cried harder than we had when we thought that she was dead. The prince asked her if she wanted to go back with him to his kingdom and she looked to us, as if she needed our permission. We could not say no. We had seen a miracle and it must have happened for a reason. We let her go and she rode off with the prince and none of us ever saw her again."

The old man bent down from his chair and picked up a small cat that had been mewing at his feet. He stroked it as it purred at him.

"And she is the one who is in danger?"

"Yes."

"Do you know where she is?"

Wexel shook his head.

"I don't. I only headed north because a voice in my head told me to."

"What sort of danger is she in?"

"The witch," answered Wexel, "she has risen out of her grave and is on her way to steal Giselle's heart."

"Like her stepmother had wanted?"

"That's right."

The old man looked down and placed the purring cat back onto the floor. His face looked sad, as if he were recalling a past regret he had not thought about in a long while.

"The people in the north are at least partly right," he sighed. "Though this forest has no more or no less thieves and murderers than any other, it does contain at least one sorcerer."

Wexel watched as the old man stood up and walked slowly to a broken-down looking cabinet. He opened it and revealed to Wexel a collection of everything a magician would need to ply his craft.

"Are you—" Wexel started to say, rising anxiously out of his chair.

"No," the old man said shaking his head. "I am not going to turn you into some small animal or do anything else to you. I simply had to tell you my profession so I could explain to you why your story is familiar to me."

He closed the cabinet and sat back down at the table. Wexel remained standing, his hand resting uneasily on the chair. He had to look up over the table to see the old man.

"There was a time," the old man explained, "when I would do whatever was asked of me as long as the coins given to me were made of real gold. I regret that now. It pains me to think how many lives I have ruined because of my greed, and it is a pain I have to live with since none of my crimes can be undone. It also pains me to know how popular my services were. I had many repeat customers, all of whom were as evil and foul as any monster you could name. The worst was a woman named Morgan whose vanity knew no contest. She was very beautiful. The most beautiful woman in all the land. And she wanted to make certain that it stayed that way.

"She came to me to enchant a mirror for her. She wanted to be able to look into it and ask who the fairest woman was and have it tell her. If she saw anything other than her own face, she would seek out her usurper and have the poor woman killed. It was a simple task and I did it for five pieces of gold, knowing that as the woman grew older more and more women would be killed to satisfy her horrible ego. I thought it might be a decade before this started happening, but it took only half that long. One morning the wicked woman looked into the mirror I had enchanted for her and asked it who the fairest woman in all the land was, and she was enraged when she saw the face of her own stepdaughter. You know what happened next.

"She called for a servant and gave him a box and said 'Take the girl to the forest and cut out her heart and place it in this box.' He was too afraid of her to refuse, but when the time came to kill the girl he couldn't do it and he let her go and instead killed a stag and placed its heart in the box Morgan had given him. He was disgusted and horrified when, in front of his eyes, she cooked and ate the heart he had given her, believing it would add to her beauty. Of course, the servant's ruse was discovered when she once again asked the mirror who the fairest in all the land was and saw Giselle's face instead of her own. She had the servant tortured and discovered that her stepdaughter was still alive in the forest. It was then that she went back to me. She asked me for poison and for a disguise. I gave her both."

The old man paused for a moment, overcome with the remembrance of a past epiphany. "But she had come to me just as I first began to question the morality of my trade. I gave her a vial of poison, but it was a poison that could be undone with an act as simple as a kiss, and I gave her a disguise, but it was one that—once worn—could never be removed. As a punishment for her wickedness, I ensured that she would—after donning the disguise—look like an ugly old woman the rest of her life. She was the one you chased to the edge of that cliff, and the miracle you witnessed was not a miracle at all, but instead the work of an old wizard taking his first steps towards his redemption."

The old man stood up and got a bottle of wine and two cups. He poured one for himself and one for Wexel and drank deeply from his. Wexel had never tried wine before because he and his brothers had never been fond of alcohol. He sipped at it and frowned. It tasted like a fruit juice that had gone horribly wrong.

"Have you any proof that Morgan has returned from the grave or did you just see her in your dream?" asked the old man while he poured himself another glass.

"I went to where she was buried. I found two men who had been killed and a hole where the rocks had once been."

The old man nodded at this before he continued.

"In your dream, did she speak at all? Did she say anything?"

"Yes," answered Wexel. "When she was buried under the rocks she kept repeating the phrase 'A little light and a little time is all I need, to make right her wretched crime, her heinous deed.'"

"Anything else?"

"After she escaped from her grave she kept saying 'Mirror calls and mirror wakes, and fairness falls and ravage takes.' "

The old man took what Wexel said in and then, slowly, he got back up and went to his cabinet.

"The spirit of the girl's stepmother is possessed by the mirror I enchanted for her," he explained, "and whoever controls the mirror, controls her. As long as the mirror exists, there is no way to stop her. And I doubt the owner of the mirror will stop with the murder of Giselle. She will use the foul old wraith to kill whoever the mirror declares is fairer than she is."

He opened the cabinet and pulled out a small wooden box.

"I was given this as payment for a spell I regret more than any other. For thirty years its presence has mocked me, but now it has a use."

He gave the box to Wexel, who looked into it. There he saw the largest and most beautiful diamond he had ever come across. Of all the thousands he had seen during his years working in the mine, he could remember only one that even came close to equaling it.

"There is only one way to make sure Morgan does not rise again and that is to shatter the mirror and plunge a piece of it into its owner's heart," explained the old man.

Wexel looked up when he heard this.

"I have to kill someone?"

"It is the only way," answered the old man. "And since the mirror is enchanted it will take a diamond like that to cut at it and weaken it enough so that it will shatter."

"Is there any way for you to tell me where the owner of the mirror is?"

The old man shook his head.

"No, but I am sure they are somewhere close to Giselle and I know where she is."

"Where?" Wexel had been waiting for this news all along.

"The kingdom of Alexia, just fifty miles east of the end of the southern forest. Once there she should be easy to find, as she has been its queen and ruler for over a decade now."

"Queen?"

"She was taken by a prince, remember. They married and for a time she was a princess, but then his father died and she became a queen. A few years ago, he died and she took over as the ruler of the kingdom."

Wexel found it almost impossible to reconcile the image of the young girl he had known with that of the regal ruler of a kingdom he had never heard of before.

"She is regarded as a wise and just leader and is much beloved by her people," the old man continued. "They should regard you as a hero if you saved her."

"I am not doing this to be a hero," Wexel insisted.

"No, I know," the old man smiled. "You are doing it for love."

• • •

Wexel's leather pack was now much heavier than it had been before he met the old man. Along with the diamond, the old wizard insisted that he take several other items that he might find useful on his journey.

"This key," the old man explained as he handed Wexel an ordinary-looking skeleton key, "will fit into and open any lock. This elixir," he said, handing Wexel a small flask, "will put anyone who drinks it into the very deepest sleep. And this dagger," he handed Wexel a very sharp and dangerous-looking knife, "is enchanted so that it can only inflict injury, but not kill."

Wexel held the dagger, which in his small hands looked like a sword, and felt a strange comfort in holding it.

"It seems an odd thing to enchant a weapon so that it cannot kill," he said to the old man.

"I give it to you because it is obvious to me that yours is not a violent heart. It will take all you have to kill the one person you must. With this dagger you will be able to defend yourself, knowing that whoever you cut with it will live to see another day."

Wexel stowed the items in his pack, along with a hand-drawn map to Alexia, and turned to leave the small shack.

"Thank you for your help," he said to the old man as he stood by the door.

"I should not be thanked for helping you clean up a mess I made," answered the old man. "Now go. You have a long way to walk and the sun is already nearly set."

Wexel left the old man and started walking in the direction indicated by the map. Though the old man had quickly jotted it down on a scrap of old parchment, it was remarkably detailed, with notes on where to camp along the way and the spots to be avoided at all costs.

He looked up into the sky and saw that the old man had been right. The sun was close to setting. He had only an hour to walk before it would become dark, and only an hour after that before it became too dark to even see. He looked at the map and found that the closest campground the old man listed on it was just a few miles away. He got there just as the sun was disappearing off the horizon. He started a small fire and cleared a spot on the ground to sleep on. As he lay on his back, he looked up into the night sky. Seeing the stars twinkle above him, he was reminded of the diamond that sat in the box in his satchel. He reached over, lifted the box out of his bag, opened it and looked at the diamond. He had been right the first time he had seen it. It *was* the most beautiful he had ever seen, but that wasn't why he had taken it out to look at it. He had taken it out, because he wanted to be reminded of the *second* most beautiful diamond he had ever seen. Reminded, he closed his eyes and remembered the moment he had given it away.

They had all lined up to say their good-byes to her. She had bent over and hugged each of them as tears streamed out of her wondrous blue eyes. He was last and when she got to him, he blushed and reached into his pocket.

"I've been saving something," he told her bashfully.

She managed to laugh and gasp at the same time.

"Wexel," she said smiling, "I didn't know you could talk!"

He shrugged.

"Yeah, I just didn't have anything to say," he admitted.

"It's so good to hear your voice!"

"Thanks," he mumbled, embarrassed. "Anyway, like I was saying, I've been saving something. I found it last year and I held onto it, because I knew it was special. I don't really deserve to have it. It's too beautiful for me, but I'd be honored if you took it. It's something you should have."

"What is it?" she asked, curious.

He took his hand out of his pocket and opened it in front of her.

She gasped wordlessly and put her hands to her cheeks.

"Wexel," she said with a stunned expression, "I can't take that. You have all already given me so much."

"Please take it," he insisted. "It would just go to waste here."

She looked down into his palm and looked at the diamond before she finally and hesitantly reached for it and took it from him.

"Thank you," she bent over and whispered to him, just before she gave him a gentle kiss on his forehead.

"You're welcome," he smiled.

A few minutes later they watched as she rode away from them, and Wexel was so sad to see her go he didn't even remember what the diamond he had given her had looked like.

But he remembered it now as he lay by the fire and its flames danced on the diamond he held in his hands. He wondered if she still had it, and he wondered if she even remembered who had given it to her.

• • •

Though he did not say it, the old man knew that there was no way for Wexel to get to Alexia in time to save Giselle. Morgan not only had a good head start on him, but the old witch could move at a speed faster than most normal men, much less a middle-aged dwarf. As he gathered a host of ingredients from out of his cabinet, he thought up every possible spell he could cast that could both slow her down and speed Wexel up. He thought of two separate spells and went to work on casting them.

The first was the hardest and required all his concentration. As he whispered a long complex chant in a language that had not been spoken aloud by anyone else for 500 years, a vaporous ball of light began to form inside his shack. Slowly it grew in mass, until it was the size and shape of a tall, strong man.

"Go forth," he ordered it when he finished chanting. "Find Wexel and stay with him until his mission has been completed."

The head of the mass of light nodded and flew out of the shack into the night, searching for Wexel.

The second spell was much easier. In fact it was so easy it required hardly any magic at all. He merely sat down and—using his mind—sent a message into the mind of someone else.

"Morgan," he told the recipient of his message, "I am the one who made you what you are. I am waiting for you."

After that he poured himself a few glasses of wine and waited.

It took her longer than he had thought it would. The sun was rising when his door smashed apart, and the old witch walked into his small shack.

"Hello, Morgan," he greeted her stoically. "I've been waiting for you."

The dead crone screamed at him and lifted him by his neck into the air. With another howl of hatred and vengeance, she lifted up her free hand and brought it down with all of her might into his chest. He screamed with pain as her hand plunged through his ribs and grabbed hold of his heart. He stopped screaming when she ripped it out of him and dropped him to the ground as if he were the foulest piece of garbage she had ever held. She then dropped his heart and turned and left the shack, having taken a significant detour away from her destination.

As she walked away she could not be bothered to turn back and take one final look at the dead man she had left to rot on the ground. If she had, she would have seen that he was smiling.

. . .

Wexel had always been a deep sleeper. His brothers used to pull all sorts of pranks on him while he was in bed, knowing that there was little they could do that would wake him. Even lying on the cold hard ground in a strange forest, this proved to be true. So he did not notice when the mass of light the old man had conjured found him and descended upon him.

The light floated over top of him and very slowly lowered itself until it encased his entire body. He felt nothing and stayed asleep. The light then began to snap and crackle as it worked its magic upon him, and this too did not awaken him. The aches and pains that resulted from the effects of the light's magic might have aroused some people, but Wexel was not one of them. In the end it took the light of the rising sun to get him to open his eyes and by that time the light had faded, its job accomplished.

Wexel felt cold as he stretched and yawned himself awake. His clothes felt so light on his body that it was as if they weren't even there at all. He sat up and nearly fainted when he saw how high the journey upward had taken him. He looked down at his legs and feet and discovered to his astonishment that the reason he felt so cold was because he was naked and the reason he was naked was because his legs and feet were now at least four or five times bigger than they had been just hours before.

Panicked, he jumped up and looked down at the tiny pile of ripped clothing that littered the ground below him. His sweater, his pants and his boots were all in tatters, unable to contain the bulk of his new body. He raised his hands and marveled at them. He made a fist and nearly wept at the size of it. As he stood there he realized the transformation wasn't purely physical as he felt a power and energy he had never known course through his body.

"Thank you, old man," he said with a smile, correctly guessing who caused his metamorphosis. "Thank you so very much."

. . .

Wexel had run before, but never like this. His new legs and body moved through the forest as if a cannon had propelled them. He had been running for hours and did not even feel tired or winded. Using the tattered remains of his clothing, he had fashioned a loincloth to cover the most intimate portions of his body, and he felt the warmth of the sun radiate all over his skin. It was a new sensation to him, one he had never allowed himself to feel before, having been too ashamed of his old body to expose it so directly to the sunlight. Now he doubted that he would ever wear clothes again. He was so proud of how he looked.

For the briefest of seconds he had allowed himself the vanity of looking at his reflection when he had stopped at a stream to get a drink of water. Though he was still bald and his face still strongly resembled the one he had always had, it would not be an exaggeration to say that he looked handsome. If before he felt anxious about seeing Giselle again, now he could not wait. No amount of magic could ever make him her equal in beauty, but he was far closer now than he had been before.

As he ran he checked his map, taking it out of the satchel that he had once struggled with and which now seemed almost comically small. After traveling for half a day he was nearing the edge of the forest, which put him just 50 miles away from Alexia, which meant he would reach the kingdom just after nightfall. Unaware of the old man's sacrifice, he feared that he might be too late. He swore to himself that if that proved to be the case, he would not stop until the person responsible died before his very eyes.

. . .

Even at night the kingdom of Alexia was unlike anything he had ever seen. It stood at the edge of a tall mountain and surrounded an enormous stone castle, which he assumed was where he would find Giselle. Instead of wood and straw, its houses were all made of brick and stone, and their owners had tried to make them look as beautiful as possible. This wasn't a squalid little village full of peasants and serfs, but a rich city whose citizens were wealthy enough to understand and appreciate the concept of luxury. He wasn't there for a minute before he became acutely embarrassed about his lack of proper clothing and knocked on the first door he saw that was marked "Tailor."

Though it was late, the owner of the shop opened the door and took in the sight of the tall, handsome and nearly naked man standing before him.

"I think you've come to the right place," the tailor said after a few awkward seconds passed.

"Before I come in," Wexel spoke to him, "can you tell me if anything has happened to the queen of this kingdom in the past few days?"

"Queen Giselle?" asked the tailor, who was a short, squat man with a round face and a messy pile of curly white hair.

"That's right."

"Nothing that I'm aware of. Why do you ask?"

"It's nothing," Wexel lied, "but I have to see her and I can't speak to her dressed like this."

"That's an understatement if I've ever heard one," laughed the tailor. "Come in, come in."

Wexel walked inside the shop. He reached into his tiny satchel and pulled out a nugget of gold.

"This is all I have to pay you with. Is that all right?"

The tailor nearly fainted when he saw the piece of glimmering metal in Wexel's hand. It was just slightly smaller than a plum.

"Son," he answered sincerely, "for that you can not only buy all the clothing I have, but this entire shop as well."

"I just need a pair of pants and a nice shirt and a tunic. Oh and do you have any shoes?"

"No, but my son's a cobbler and he lives just next door. I'll go get him."

The excited little man ran out of his store and returned three minutes later with a young and confused-looking man in an apron. The confusion vanished from the man's face when he caught sight of the gold in Wexel's hand. He ran back out of the house and returned with his arms filled with shoes.

"I don't know what to look for," Wexel told the men, "so could you pick for me?"

A few minutes later Wexel was dressed in clothes so fine anyone who looked at him would be shocked to learn he was not of noble blood. Among the items the men had chosen for him were a pair of soft black leather boots that went to his knees, black cotton pants, a white silk shirt, a dark red embroidered tunic, black leather gloves and—to complete the ensemble—a hooded black cloak. The cloak had several pockets sewn into it, so he emptied his small satchel and filled them with his supplies. When he was finished he stood in front of the two men.

"Do I look good enough for the queen?" he asked them.

They both smiled and nodded.

• • •

The guard standing at the gate at the end of the castle's drawbridge was nodding off when Wexel approached him. He had to politely cough to get the man's attention.

"What business have you here?" asked the man, annoyed to have his nap disturbed.

"I am here to see the queen," answered Wexel.

"So what else is new?" asked the guard.

"It is very important," Wexel insisted. "Her life depends on it."

The guard yawned.

"You have a name?"

"Wexel. I am an old friend of the queen's. I knew her when she was just a girl."

The guard rolled his eyes at this and called over another guard, who was trying to nap in the castle's courtyard. The other guard yawned wearily, got up and walked over to them. The guard at the gate turned to him and spoke.

"Tell Jerome that there's a guy named Weasel—"

"Wexel—"

"Right—Wexel—who wants to see the queen. Says he knew her when she was a girl."

The other guard nodded at this and walked away.

"Who's Jerome?" asked Wexel.

"The queen's head servant," answered the guard. "He's the one who decides who gets to see the queen."

"Oh."

A half hour passed before the guard came back with a tall, lean man with thinning gray hair and an air of hostile authority. The man was obviously annoyed to be disturbed, but he changed his attitude when he caught sight of the noble-looking gentleman standing in front of him.

"You're a stranger to me, sir," the man said to him. "I do not think you have ever been here before."

"You're right. I haven't," Wexel admitted.

"Then what business could you possibly have with our queen?"

"I have learned that she is in mortal danger."

"How so?"

"It would be best if I explained it all to her."

"Really? Why is that?"

"Because it is a strange story. One that she will know enough to accept, but that will strike others as impossible."

Jerome looked Wexel up and down with a studied eye.

"All right," he decided. "I will take you to her, but she alone will decide if she will let you speak."

At this the guard at the gate pulled a lever and the gate rose and Wexel walked into the castle's courtyard and followed the servant towards the castle.

"I should warn you," Jerome said, turning to him as they walked, "the queen gets many visitors and has little time to hear what they all have to say."

"She will want to talk to me," Wexel insisted confidently.

• • •

It happened so quickly. Wexel wasn't even prepared for it. Jerome opened a door and there she was, sitting in a chair reading from a pile of documents. Seeing her knocked the wind out of his lungs, and he felt as though he was going to pass out. He was so overcome to see her that it took him a moment to realize that his dream had been wrong. She had changed since he had saw her last, and no longer looked like the girl he had known 30 years ago. This, however, did not mean her beauty had lessened. If anything she was more beautiful than he remembered. Age had given her face a wisdom and maturity it had not had before, and the effect was dizzying to behold. But her timeless beauty alone would not have been enough to affect him so deeply. What had moved him even more was that—embedded in a choker around her neck—was the diamond he had given her all those years ago. She still had it and he prayed that she remembered who had given it to her.

"What is it, Jerome?" she asked without looking up from the papers she was reading. "I'm very busy."

"This gentleman requests a moment of your time," answered Jerome. "He insists that he has news about your life being in danger."

She looked up and studied the tall, handsome stranger in front of her.

"What is your name?" she asked him directly.

"Wexel, your majesty," he answered her, having finally regained his breath.

She paused, as if his answer reminded her of a distant memory.

"That is an odd name," she said to him, as her hand reached up to touch the diamond that sat at her neck.

"Yes it is, your majesty," he admitted.

"But what is even odder is that you are not the first person I have met with that name."

He could not help smiling.

"Yes I am, your majesty. I can guarantee that I am the only person you have ever met named Wexel."

This made her cross.

"That is a very arrogant thing to say," she chastised him. "How dare you tell me who I have and haven't met!"

"I meant no disrespect, your majesty," he apologized, "but I stand by my statement. I am the only person named Wexel you have ever met."

Something about how he said this caused the queen to put down her papers and get up and approach him. She walked slowly towards him, and he stood up as straight as he could and returned her steady gaze. Finally, when she stood just a foot from him, he smiled again and she looked deeply into his eyes. She gasped when she realized he was telling the truth. He was the only person she had ever met with that name.

"But how?" she marveled at him.

"I met up with an old wizard in the northern forest," he explained. "When I told him of the danger I knew you were in, he enchanted me so I could help save you."

It was too much for her to believe and she held herself back.

"I see you have kept my gift," he said. "I don't think you could ever know how much that means to me."

Once again she reached up and touched her diamond and then—to the shocked surprise of Jerome who watched what was happening with a look of utter confusion—she threw herself into Wexel's arms and gave him a long, hard hug.

"I never thought I'd see you again," she laughed and cried at the same time.

"Me too," he hugged her back.

She let him go and held him at arm's length and admired what he had become.

"How are your brothers?" she asked him.

"Gone," he said sadly.

Her face saddened and she let him go.

"All of them?"

"Yes."

"I'm so sorry. I thought of you all so often over the years."

"And we thought of you."

"I'm glad to hear it," she said smiling. "Now explain to me what it is that is happening that a magician would see fit to cause this miraculous transformation of yours."

"Your life is in danger, your majesty," he spoke urgently. "Just a few days ago I had a dream in which I saw the spirit of the witch who first tried to murder you return from her grave and find you and take that which she had always wanted."

The queen gently placed her right hand upon her chest.

"My heart?" she asked, her voice barely above a whisper.

"Yes," he nodded. "The dream was unlike any I had ever experienced before. It was so real I got up from my bed and walked to where I knew the witch had been buried. There I found a hole in the ground and two dead men beside it. On instinct I went into the northern forest and found a wizard who told me what was happening and what I had to do to stop it. He told me that the foul spirit of your stepmother could only be stopped by killing the person who now owns and controls her enchanted mirror."

"And who could this be?" she asked him.

"I don't know," he admitted. "But I was thinking as I ran to Alexia. It occurred to me that whoever possesses the mirror must be using it for the same reason as your stepmother, which means that they are both beautiful and extremely vain. They have targeted you because your beauty is still the greatest in the land and they cannot bear it. I hoped that the people of your kingdom are goodhearted enough that such a person would be easy to find among them."

"I think you are right," said the queen. "I can think of few in Alexia capable of such horrible narcissism." She walked back up to him and gave him another hug. "It is so good to see you again," she told him, "and I am very grateful for your efforts to warn me about your dream. Thankfully I have a whole army of guards to protect me, so I think it is safe for me to get some sleep tonight. And you as well. I'm sure your journey has been hard. Jerome will take you to a room where you will find a warm comfortable bed to sleep in."

Wexel didn't like how she underplayed the danger she was in. He tried to protest, but she interrupted him before he could get the words out.

"Do not worry, my dear friend," she said. "I have no plans on dying any time soon, but you must understand that my life has been endangered before and if I panicked every time I would have lost my sanity long ago."

He stayed quiet, forced to admit to himself that he couldn't comprehend the life she had lived since he had seen her last. Jerome turned to leave and he followed after them. When they stepped into the hallway, the queen called out to them.

"Jerome, could you please come in here for a moment?" she said. "I have a private matter to discuss with you."

The tall servant turned back and listened as the queen whispered a few words in his ear. Wexel couldn't hear what she was saying. When she was finished, Jerome looked at her and bowed and walked back out of the room.

"Right this way," he said to Wexel as he began to walk down the hallway.

Wexel followed Jerome as he turned down a long and winding stairway. There were only a few lamps lit along the way and it was very dark. Wexel assumed he was being taken to the servants' quarters. He didn't mind. He figured their beds still had to be better than the one he had at home. They finally reached the bottom of the stairs, and Wexel was shocked to see a fat, drunken man sitting with a dog in front of five small prison cells.

"Why did we come here?" he asked Jerome when he realized it was the castle's dungeon.

The servant answered him by bringing a heavy leather strap filled with sand against the back of his head. Wexel fell dazed to one knee, and Jerome hit him once again. Wexel saw a bright flash of light and then total darkness. He fell hard against the ground and Jerome walked back upstairs. The jailer went through all of the pockets he could find in Wexel's cloak and took whatever was in them. He was rewarded for his efforts with a couple of nuggets of gold, a flask, a key, a dagger and—most importantly—a box that contained an awe-inspiring diamond. Thrilled beyond all knowing, he dragged Wexel into the closest cell and slammed the door shut.

• • •

Wexel awoke with an agonizing pain throbbing throughout his skull. It hurt so much he could barely put in the effort it took to comprehend what had happened to him. The pieces did not fit. He could not believe that Giselle would do this to him, but then here he was. His injured brain did somersaults as it tried to explain why she would hurt him, when it suddenly occurred to him that she wasn't the one responsible. It had to be the servant, Jerome! The devious usurper was planning a palace coup and was using the mirror to make it happen! He was the one who controlled Morgan's spirit and the one that had to be stopped!

"Jailer!" Wexel jumped up and shouted anxiously through the barred opening on his prison door. "You have to let me out! If you don't the queen will die!"

The fat man couldn't even be bothered to look up at him.

"Sit down," the man grunted as he sat and admired the diamond he had stolen from Wexel.

"Listen to me! Jerome is planning to kill the queen and you are helping him!"

With a sigh the jailer stood and lifted up a heavy cane and slammed it hard against Wexel's right hand, which had been wrapped around one of the heavy iron bars. Wexel howled with pain and stepped back from the door. He could tell immediately that at least two of his fingers had been broken.

"Sit down," the jailer repeated before he went back to his chair.

Wexel stayed quiet and racked his brain for ways to get out of this horrible situation. He looked around his cell and was horrified to find that he shared the space with a decaying skeleton. He knew then he could not reason with the man, because someone who couldn't even be bothered to dispose of the dead would have little compassion for the living.

He searched through his cloak to see if there were any items the man had not stolen. The only thing he found was the length of rope he had used to scale down the cliff that separated the two halves of the forest. It had seemed so strong and sturdy when he used it then, but now in his transformed hands it looked like what it essentially was—a length of particularly strong twine. Cautiously, he once again approached his door and took a quick and silent look. He saw the jailer sitting on his chair with everything he had stolen lined up on the small table beside him. Wexel stepped back and began to formulate a plan. He prayed that it would work, fearing more for what would happen to the queen if he failed than what would happen to himself.

"Hey!" he shouted through his door. "The least you can do is let me have my whiskey back!"

The jailer looked at him and snorted with laughter.

"Is that what's in here?" the fat man grinned as he lifted up the flask from the table.

"The finest I ever drank," Wexel insisted. "I'm dying for another taste."

"Well," the man laughed, "if it's so good why would I waste it on a pissant like you?"

"Because you have a good heart?"

This statement caused the man to rock forward with a huge gut-bursting gale of laughter. When he was finished he opened the flask and lifted it to his lips and took a drink. His smiled vanished almost instantly as the effects of the elixir took hold of him and all consciousness left his body. He dropped the flask and most of his contents splashed out onto the floor. His other hand fell as well and dropped the diamond, which he had not let go of. Wexel watched with horror as the man's dog walked over to the diamond, sniffed it and then picked it up with its mouth and swallowed it whole. The animal coughed for a full minute as it choked down the hefty jewel. When it finally got it down, it walked over to the part of the floor that was wet from spilled elixir and licked it. A few seconds later it too was out unconscious on the floor.

Wexel then unrolled the rope and looked around his cell for a nail or something he could tie the rope to. After several minutes, he concluded that there was nothing to be found. Out of desperation he went to the body of the dead man and went through its clothes. The skeleton's pockets were empty, probably because the jailer had cleaned the man out before he had thrown him in. Wexel's heart began to race as he tried to figure out what he could do. For a second he looked down at the skeleton and noticed that its hands seemed strangely gnarled and calcified. Wexel remembered seeing men in the various villages around the old cabin whose hands looked like that. When he was young he had once asked one man what was wrong with them, and the man had told him that they had "Turned to stone."

Having no other option, he bent over and used all of his strength to snap off the index finger on the skeleton's right hand. He tied it to the end of the rope and walked over to the door and threw the bone towards the table where his enchanted key was sitting. It took him several attempts to reach the table, and a few more to get near the key, but eventually he was able to drag the key off the table, where it clattered on the floor. After that he spent a long and frustrating hour getting the key closer and closer to his cell door, until finally—just when the effort of it all was about to claim his patience and his sanity—he got it close enough that he could reach for it from under the crack beneath his door. He was so impatient to get it that he reached for it with his right hand and howled once again as the pain from his two broken fingers jolted throughout his body. Somehow, despite the pain, he was able to grab it.

He shouted with joy and relief when he got it into his cell, but his celebration ended when he tried to get it into the lock outside his door. He tried both arms, but his two broken fingers made his right arm useless and no matter how hard he tried he could not reach it with his left. Tears of frustration began to cloud his eyes until he realized what he had to do. He stopped and took off the leather glove he wore on his left hand. He folded it into two and placed it between his teeth and bit it very hard. He then reached his arm out through the door once again and began to stretch. When his arm painfully began to insist that it could go no farther, he ignored it and stretched some more. He bit even harder on his glove and felt his body scream out in agony as his shoulder slowly began to pop out of its socket. The pain was so intense he wanted to faint, but he stayed conscious and somehow—through some superhuman effort he had never known was in him—managed to keep hold of the key and slip it into the lock. Another furious jolt of pain rocketed inside him as he turned the key, but his suffering was rewarded when he heard a click and the door opened.

Exhausted, he fell to the floor and wept. He wanted to stay there, but he knew he couldn't. Slowly he raised himself from the ground. His left arm dangled from his shoulder as if it belonged on a rag doll. Years ago he had watched as his oldest brother Elias helped reset his brother Littleton's dislocated shoulder, and recalling the memory, he started to look around the dungeon for something heavy to lift. He looked down at the unconscious jailer and figured that the fat man was his best option. He picked up the leather glove he had bit on from where it had dropped when he fell, and placed it once again between his teeth. He bit down on it, bent over and grabbed the fat man by his belt with his dangling left hand. He stood up and the full weight of the man pulled down on his arm. Wexel screamed louder than he ever thought he could with clenched teeth. The pain of resetting his shoulder was even worse than dislocating it in the first place. His arm popped back into place and tears of pain streamed down his cheeks. His entire body roared at him with rage over what he had just put it through, but at least his arm was back where it was supposed to be.

When his brain finally got past the pain and started thinking clearly again, he tore some strips off the jailer's shirt and used them to tie his two broken fingers together. He then grabbed his gold and his enchanted dagger from the table where the jailer had put them, and he bent over to see if any elixir was left in the flask. He saw that there was just enough to use on one other person. He grabbed the key from the floor and was about to leave when he realized the diamond he needed was somewhere inside the large unconscious dog lying at the jailer's feet. He considered the idea of cutting the dog open and getting it back, but realized that the knife he had was incapable of such a feat. Such cuts would invariably prove deadly, and his dagger was incapable of inflicting fatal damage. It then occurred to him that he could kill the dog with a rock, and then get the diamond, as he presumed the knife would have no problem cutting through flesh that was already dead. Then he remembered that around the queen's neck was a diamond almost as good. He would simply ask her to lend it to him so he could use it to destroy the mirror.

Having figured this out, he turned out of the dungeon and ran up the long winding stairway that led to the upper part of the castle. He was halfway up it when he realized it had been a mistake to run up it. His body was so sore and exhausted it did not have the energy to move that fast. His steps grew slower and slower, until finally he fell forward and had to crawl up them on his hands and knees. It took him forever to reach the door at the top, and when he did he opened it and collapsed.

As he lay there helplessly he felt certain that he was losing his mind. He knew this because before his eyes he saw Giselle—not the older queen he had just seen hours before, but the young girl he had known three decades earlier. She was dressed in clothes that could barely be described as rags, and she looked down at him with a look of horror and pity.

She spoke to him, but he did not respond because he knew she was a hallucination. Instead he closed his eyes and felt himself drift off somewhere far away.

• • •

He felt something cold and wet touch his forehead. It felt good. He opened his eyes and discovered that he was still in the midst of a hallucination. He saw Giselle—young Giselle—washing his face with a wet cloth. He lay on a small bed in a tiny and cold stone room with a dirt floor and not a single window to let in light.

"You're awake," she spoke to him, her face illuminated by the one candle that was the room's only light.

"No," he insisted. "I'm dreaming. This has to be a dream."

"Why do you say that?"

"Because you're here and you can't be. You aren't real."

"That's news to me."

"But I saw you. You look older. You're still beautiful, but you look older."

She lifted the cloth and looked at him.

"Are you talking about the queen?" she asked him.

He nodded.

"Yes. I have seen the old Giselle, so I know the young one cannot exist," he answered her.

She smiled at this, amused by his confusion.

"What is it?" he asked her.

"The queen, or Giselle—as you called her—is my mother. I am her daughter, Regine."

Wexel looked at the girl and could not believe it. Yes, she looked just like Giselle, but her dirty clothes were not those that belonged on a princess. Her face and arms were covered with dirt and she looked as though she was the lowest of all household servants.

"But—" he began as he attempted to express these thoughts with words, but the girl read his mind and interrupted him before he could get them out.

"Three years ago," she explained, "my father died and something happened to my mother. I don't know what it was, but she changed. She became cruel and mean and eventually she refused to acknowledge my existence. Whenever someone asked about me, she acted as though she had never had a child. Finally, the court accepted her madness as law and I ceased to be Princess Regine and was sent here to this room and treated like a worthless servant. Since then no one here has talked to me for fear that they might anger my mother."

Wexel stared at her as he tried to accept this. The girl's story explained both her uncanny resemblance to the Giselle he once knew and the way she was dressed, but he could not believe that Giselle would be capable of doing something so insane and cruel.

"There is no way—" he stammered. "She wouldn't do such a thing."

"She did," the girl quietly insisted, her voice filled with the resignation of someone forced long ago to accept her fate. "I wish I could explain it, but I can't. I remember when she was kind and loving and treated me as though I was her most important gift in the world."

"And then?"

"My father died and her heart was broken. From that point on she spent hours each day in her room, staring at herself in her mirror."

Regine watched as what she said appeared to trigger something in the mind of the tall, handsome stranger on her bed. She might as well have slapped him to get such a reaction. She watched as a sudden and obvious epiphany exploded in his mind, and she sat quietly as the force of it reduced him to tears. Whatever she had said, it had been something the man needed to hear.

"I had a dream," he explained through his tears. "I thought I had it so I could save her, but I didn't. I had it so I could save you."

"I don't understand."

"Your mother," he wept, "she has awakened a foul witch and has sent her here to take your heart. You have become the fairest of all the land and for it, she wants you dead."

"But who are you?" she asked him. "Why would you dream such a thing?"

"Because we saved her. She would not be here if it were not for us."

"Why do you say 'we'?"

"My brothers. We saved her and cared for her and were too blinded by her beauty to ever see what she might some-day become."

Before Regine could say anything, the sound of loud screams echoed above them.

"She's here!" Wexel sat up. "She's coming for you."

"Who?"

"Morgan," he told her as a sudden burst of adrenaline allowed him to jump to his feet from the bed. "Your step-grandmother. She is coming for your heart." He ran and closed the door to the small room. "There is no time to run. There is nowhere we can go."

The screams grew louder as the horrible crone easily made her way past the castle's guards. She would find them in only a manner of a few minutes.

Wexel stood quiet and still and tried to think of what he could possibly do. He reached into his cloak's pockets, hoping for inspiration and he found it when his hand touched the flask that contained the elixir that had knocked out the jailer and his dog. He handed it to Regine.

"Drink this," he ordered. "I hope there is enough."

"What is it?" she asked him.

"Just drink it!" he shouted. "We have no time!"

She looked scared, but she listened to him and drank the last few drops of the elixir. It was enough. She fell to the ground in a heap, and Wexel lifted her up and placed her on her bed. He then took out his enchanted dagger and held it above her heart.

"Please," he prayed. "Please."

He brought down the dagger as hard as he could. It cut easily through the bone, and he could feel it slash into her heart. He let it go and it stayed there.

The screams were so loud now it was obvious the creature was only a few seconds away. Wexel turned and blew out the candle, plunging the room into total darkness. He wrapped his dark cloak around him and ran to a corner and stood there as quietly as he could. And just like before, when he had hid from the magician in the hollowed out tree, he became aware of just how loud he was when he wanted to be completely silent.

The door to the room burst open. The crone stood in the doorway, covered in the blood of all the men she had killed to get there.

"Mirror calls and mirror wakes," she cackled, "and fairness falls and ravage takes!"

Light from the hallway shone through the doorway and with it the old witch saw Regine, lying lifelessly on her bed. She moved carefully toward the girl and howled with anger when she saw the knife sticking out of Regine's chest.

"Take it!" a voice ordered the creature from outside the room. "What are you waiting for? Take it!"

The creature turned. There was nothing it could do.

Giselle walked into the room.

"I want her heart!" she demanded.

"It," the witch's words came out in a slow deliberate hiss, "is already destroyed."

Giselle looked down at the body of her daughter.

"She killed herself," she smiled. "I might have guessed she would do that." This appeared to amuse her. "I suppose there was never any need to send those men out to dig you up and order you to come here, but," she decided, "now that you're here, I'm sure I'll find other uses for you."

With that she turned and walked out of the room.

The creature looked down one last time at the girl on the bed and then turned and looked around the room. Wexel stayed completely still as he stood in the corner. The witch's eyes did not see him because his black cloak remained hidden by the darkness. She turned and followed the queen out of the room.

Wexel waited for several minutes before he decided it was safe. He moved away from the corner and ran to Regine. Carefully, he slid the knife from out of her chest and watched as the wound closed instantly, as if the knife had never touched her. He looked down at the dagger and saw that there was no blood at all on its blade. Instead, all he saw was his own reflection.

"You're a fool," he told himself. "And you've got one last thing you have to do."

• • •

Giselle had received the mirror as a gift from her husband. He had brought it back from his last trip to the kingdoms of the southern forest. Over the years he had given her so many presents she had little space in her room to keep them all, so she had developed the habit of keeping them stored in another room and rotating them in and out of her own. She kept up this habit even after the king died when he was accidentally thrown from his horse during a morning ride. It was a month after his death that she found the mirror in the storage room and took it and hung it up on her wall. The first time she looked into it, she was amazed by what she saw. She had never been vain before, but at that moment she was struck by the power of her beauty. She couldn't help but stare at herself. She became awed by her own reflection and she found herself asking the mirror who the fairest woman in all the land was, and every time she did she saw her own reflection.

But then she noticed how much her daughter Regine was starting to resemble herself when she was a young woman. She knew it would only be a matter of time before the mirror gave her a different answer. The thought of it turned her heart cold. She began to ignore her daughter and pretended the young girl did not exist. It didn't take long for her people and servants to get the point. They too joined in her denial, and Regine was forced to live only slightly better than an animal in the castle's basement. For a time this was enough to keep Giselle satisfied, but then one horrible night she asked the mirror the question and instead of her own face, she saw Regine's instead.

She had screamed when she saw it, but she calmed down within seconds. The mirror spoke to her. Not with words, but she understood it all the same. She listened and followed its orders. She sent two men to where her stepmother had been buried and waited for the dead witch to return and take Regine's heart. She had not counted on the return of the dwarf. She feared that the magic that had transformed him would be enough to stop her, but that proved to not be the case. Regine was now dead. Her death meant she could once again stand in front of the mirror and ask it the question whose answer was important enough that both she and her stepmother had been willing to kill for it. She stood in front of it and closed her eyes as she said the words.

"Mirror, mirror, on the wall," she smiled, "who's the fairest one of all?"

She opened her eyes, expecting to see her own reflection. Instead, she once again saw the innocent face of her young and tortured daughter.

"No!" she screamed at the mirror. "She's dead! This cannot be!"

"Sure it can," spoke a familiar voice behind her.

The image of her daughter faded and now in the mirror she could see that the stupid overgrown dwarf was standing behind her.

"How did you—" she began to ask, but Wexel did not give her time to finish. He ran to her and grabbed the choker she wore around her neck. She screamed for help, but all of her guards were dead, victims of her stepmother's wrath. Realizing this she called out to Morgan, who appeared at her door as the dwarf began to cut at the mirror with the diamond in his hand.

"Kill him!" she ordered the creature.

Her stepmother started to move towards him, but she stopped when the dwarf began to speak.

"Before you kill me, Morgan," he said, "ask yourself if this is what you want, to be subservient to the girl who made you what you are today, old, dead and very, very ugly. Or would you prefer to watch her die, knowing that when she does you can be given what you never had, a decent and dignified burial?"

Giselle was horrified to see that the foul creature actually appeared to be pondering the dwarf's question.

"What are you doing?" she shouted. "Kill him! Now! I command you!"

The witch looked at the two people in front of her and made her decision.

Giselle screamed as her stepmother grabbed her and held her tightly in her cold, cold arms. She struggled and fought against the dead witch, but she could not escape from her grasp.

Wexel cut away at the mirror with the diamond until finally it was ready to be broken. He lifted it off the wall and smashed it against the floor. Giselle screamed as it shattered and hundreds of shards scattered at their feet. Wexel bent over and picked up the longest, sharpest shard that he could find. She looked at him and saw that there were tears in his eyes.

"You're pathetic," she insulted him.

"I know," he admitted as he lifted the shard and drove it into her heart.

• • •

Wexel woke up on the glass-covered floor. Somehow he was not cut. He closed his eyes again and remembered the flash of light that had exploded in the room the instant he had killed Giselle. He opened them again and turned his head and saw her and Morgan both lying dead on the floor. He sat up and immediately noticed how much quicker the trip took him. He sighed and looked at his hand. It was very small. He looked down and saw that his shirt had become a blanket and his feet didn't even make it to the waist of his pants. His mission was completed, and the spell that had transformed him had ended

He did not feel sad. He felt relieved. He felt normal. The way he should be. He stood up, leaving his cloak and his pants and boots on the floor. His white shirt and tunic hung down to his ankles. He took off the heavy tunic and dropped it onto the floor. He saw the choker with the diamond on it and bent over and picked it up.

The castle was eerily quiet. All those who were not dead had run away, and it could be hours or even days before any of them returned. He walked down to the lowest part of the castle and found Regine's room. She was still there, lying unconscious on her bed. He walked over to her and gave her a gentle shake, hoping it would wake her. He was horrified to discover how cold she felt. He felt for a pulse and found nothing. He placed his hand over her lips and felt no breath.

"What have I done?" he asked himself. He couldn't believe that he had gone through so much, only to fail. Not only had he failed, but also he himself was responsible for her death. Something must have gone wrong with the dagger. It must have destroyed her heart. The thought of this was too much for him to take, and his face collapsed down into his arms. He had no more tears to weep and wanted only to die himself.

"I'm sorry, Regine," he whispered. "If my brothers were here I would help them make you the finest casket in the world, but they're not, so I can't."

Somehow he found the strength to stand back up and he started to walk away, when the memory of what had happened 30 years before flooded into his mind. He paused and wondered. The old man had given Morgan the poison she had used all those years ago, knowing its effects could be undone. Wexel turned back towards Regine, praying that the magician had done it once again.

He had to stand on his tiptoes to reach her lips. The kiss was the gentlest the world had ever known. When it was over he closed his eyes and waited.

"What happened?" he heard a voice whisper below him.

He opened his eyes and saw that she was awake.

"Who are you?" she asked him.

He started to explain, but she stopped him.

"No, I know who you are. You look different now. Like the way you should."

He smiled at this.

"That's very kind of you to say."

"It's true," she insisted. "What happened?" she asked again.

"You're safe," he answered her.

"Am I?"

"Yes."

She sat up.

"Where is my mother?"

"Dead."

"Oh."

"That means you're now the queen," he told her.

She shook her head.

"No. I am just a servant girl no one ever dared to look at or talk to. I cannot be their queen. Not now."

"Then where will you go? What will you do?"

"I don't know."

Wexel paused. He didn't know if he had the right to say what he was about to say.

"There is a cabin," he spoke quietly. "It sits in the southern part of the forest. It's quiet there and very few people ever come by to visit."

"It sounds nice."

"It is."

"Will you be there?"

"Yes."

"Good."

• • •

On the way back they followed the map the old man had given him. The trip took longer than it had before. His little legs could only walk a quarter of the distance his larger ones had. Despite their languid pace, Regine looked happy and serene. The forest was new to her and she loved it.

"This feels like home," she told him just before they reached the cliff that separated the two halves of the forest. They used a rope to climb it, and a few hours later they walked into the empty cabin. Wexel made a stew and the two of them ate happily together.

When they were finished, Wexel asked Regine to join him outside.

"There are some people I want you to meet."

She followed him, and he introduced her to his brothers.

"This is Regine," he told them. "She's going to be living with us, for as long as she likes."

"Hello," Regine greeted them with a shy smile.

Wexel could tell that they approved.

The months passed quickly after that and as the seasons changed, Wexel waited for Regine to grow bored or for a handsome stranger to appear on a horse from out of nowhere. But she never did, and the handsome stranger never arrived. The two lived together until one night Wexel went to sleep and didn't wake up. Regine buried him beside his brothers.

She was now alone and—knowing what had happened to the last of the seven brothers—she waited patiently for the day when a dream would tell her where it was she had to go.

Business as Usual

LLOYD HAD NEVER SEEN MR. KAUFMAN so enraged in all of the 10 years he had spent working at the Wichita home office of McQueen Comestibles Incorporated. The older man's face was a dark scarlet mask of anger and—somehow—Lloyd was the person responsible for provoking it into being. He stood quietly and tried not to shake as his boss screamed at him apocalyptically for an obviously serious but thus far unnamed breach of office etiquette.

"You think you're hilarious, don't you?" Mr. Kaufman shouted at him rhetorically. "You think that just because you're married to the owner's daughter that you can get away with all of your juvenile little pranks! Well, let me set the record straight, because you're greatly mistaken! This kind of behavior simply won't stand! You hear me! I don't care who you think you are, you do this again and you're out! No ifs, no ands, no buts—OUT!"

Lloyd—taken aback by the ferocity of this outburst—mumbled a quick apology before he turned heel and ran out of the furious executive's office. He still had no idea what he had done to deserve such a passionate rebuke. His heart pounded in his chest as he walked back to his small office, even though he knew that his boss' threats were empty. The truth was that, precisely because he was married to the owner's daughter, there was no way he could get fired, no matter what Kaufman said. In fact, it was only a matter of time before the older man would be put out to pasture and Lloyd would take his place in the large office with the panoramic view of lovely downtown Wichita. Perhaps that was why Kaufman was so angry. Maybe he sensed that his end was near.

By the time Lloyd sat back down in his chair, he had managed to calm himself. He wasn't there for three seconds before Kevin, who worked in the office across from his, walked in and shook his head with a chuckle.

"Sometimes I don't know how you get away with it," he laughed.

"What are you talking about?" asked Lloyd.

"What am I talking about?" Kevin asked. "Your apparent death wish is what I'm talking about. Did you really think he'd let something like that pass?"

"I obviously must have, because I have no clue about what it is I supposedly did."

"You're kidding me, right?"

"I swear to God," Lloyd answered sincerely.

Kevin went back to his office and grabbed a blue duotang folder from off his desk. He handed it to Lloyd, who shrugged.

"This is the report I handed in yesterday," he said, confused.

"Have you read it?" asked Kevin.

"Of course, I did. I wrote the useless thing."

"Then can you tell me what you were thinking when you wrote the third paragraph on page seven?"

Lloyd frowned and turned to page seven and read the third paragraph. Having written the report he expected to find the following:

While sales of our line of gluten-free cinnamon sticky-buns have increased dramatically since their introduction last year, they have yet to grow enough for me to suggest that we continue production. I think we overestimated the demand for such a product among those who suffer from Celiac Disease, and it would be in our best interests to refocus our attentions on our regular sticky-bun line, which has thus far proved consistently profitable.

So he was more than a little bit surprised when he instead read:

Despite all human notions of logic, sales of our line of gluten-free cinnamon sticky-buns have increased somewhat since they were introduced—despite my objections—last year. I take some delight, though, in writing that these sales are not nearly good enough for me to suggest that we continue producing this idiotic product. Did we really think there were enough people in this world that actually care if their sticky-buns have gluten in them or not? I say we dump this loser and stop fooling around with this kind of nonsense.

Lloyd couldn't believe his eyes. No wonder Mr. Kaufman had been so angry. His son suffered from Celiac Disease and the gluten-free sticky-buns had been his pet project. Lloyd had taken a risk just suggesting that they discontinue the line, but never in a million years would he have phrased his opinion so bluntly.

He turned to his computer and opened the file that contained the report. He scrolled down to page seven and saw that his original version of the paragraph was still in place. He then turned to his filing cabinet and found the original printout and discovered that it too contained his much more diplomatic paragraph.

In his mind he went over every detail about what had happened the previous day. He remembered finishing the report, printing it, photocopying it, collating it into separate folders and then, finally, handing out those folders around the office. He had been with the report every step of the way, and there hadn't been a single moment during which the switch could have been made.

"Is this the report I handed you?" he asked Kevin.

"Yep," Kevin nodded with a bemused smile.

"Are you positive?"

"Sure I am. I remember spilling some coffee on it when you gave it to me. You can still see the stain on the front cover."

Lloyd checked the cover of the report. The coffee stain was still there.

"How could this have happened?" he wondered aloud.

"What are you talking about?" asked Kevin.

"I didn't write this," he insisted.

"Seriously?"

"Seriously. Even I'm not this reckless."

"Then who did it?"

"That's just it. No one could have. They wouldn't have had the chance."

"Well, obviously that's not true. It happened, so they must have gotten to it somehow."

"Yeah, but even if they did, why would they do it?"

"Are you kidding?" asked Kevin.

"No. Why would you say that?"

"It's just a strange question to hear from the guy who brought down Irwin Curtis."

"That was different."

"How?"

Lloyd thought about this for a second.

"I don't know. It just was," was the best he could come up with.

• • •

Irwin Curtis was one of those people it was nearly impossible to like. Sarcastic, obnoxious and incapable of even the simplest acts of kindness or generosity, he was a porcine disaster of a man. He stood barely five feet tall, but he weighed well over 200 pounds. He moved slowly and could be heard from many feet away as he snorted and puffed his way through the office. Balding, he styled his hair into a comb-over so self-deluded that it inspired awe in all those who saw it for the first time. His nonexistent sense of sartorial style allowed him to wear the cheapest suits he could find, regardless of how poorly they fit or the pain they inflicted on other people's senses. In short, he was the type of man who was destined to spend his entire life in mid-management. Too corrupt and heartless to remain at the bottom, he was also too irritating and uncouth to get to the top, so once he was promoted to the position of Assistant to the Vice-President in Charge of Marketing and Production, he had reached the pinnacle of his corporate career.

Like everyone else at McQueen Comestibles, Lloyd had come to loath the man, even though they had never so much as said hello to each other in all the time he had worked there. But, unlike the others who tried their best to disguise their true feelings for the man, Lloyd openly derided Irwin every chance he got. He did it both behind Irwin's back and to his face (although his digs were often subtle enough that they went unnoticed). Though his hostility was genuine, Lloyd had another reason for his constant attacks. He coveted Irwin's position at the company and had decided to do whatever he had to in order to get it.

The problem was that as awful as Irwin was as a human being, he was damn good at his job, and as long as this was the case Lloyd's constant insults and petty slanders were as effective in getting Irwin fired as trying to sink an oil tanker by shooting at it with a bb gun. Lloyd knew that if he was to be successful he had to do more than point out Irwin's personal flaws. He was going to have to sabotage the man's work.

While he waited for the right opportunity to make his move against his chosen enemy, he leapt upon another opportunity by courting the company's attractive young receptionist, Scarlet. Despite her quick wit and healthy blonde good looks, Lloyd hadn't asked her out because he thought she was pretty or fun to be with. Instead he had focused in on her because she happened to be the daughter of Imogene McQueen, the founder and owner of McQueen Comestibles.

Mrs. McQueen had founded the company after her husband, Franklin, had passed away. In the beginning all she had was a recipe for oatmeal cookies that all of her friends insisted was so good she should package and sell them to supermarkets. Using the bulk of her savings she did exactly that and through a variety of miracles and lucky breaks she managed to avoid instantaneous bankruptcy and instead made money right away. Her small company grew and grew, until finally it was large enough to go public. She retained 51% of the company's shares but relinquished day-to-day control to a board of governors. Still, the company was run her way, and it was no big secret that the board didn't do anything without her explicit approval. So it didn't take much brainpower to figure out that getting to know her and getting in her good books was a surefire way to move up in the company. The easiest way for Lloyd to do that was to date her daughter.

Luckily he turned out to actually like Scarlet, who reciprocated his affections. Mrs. McQueen heartily approved of him and with her blessing he proposed to her daughter six months after they had started dating. The wedding was large and lavish, and after it and the long honeymoon in paradise were over, he was in a perfect position to make his move and get Irwin out of his way.

Unfortunately, Irwin was such a naturally suspicious and devious person that it was incredibly difficult to do anything sneaky around him or to him. Frustrated, Lloyd decided that if the annoying little man wouldn't give him an opening, he would have to make one himself.

Anita Asland, the young woman who had replaced Scarlet as the company's receptionist, looked as though she had stepped out of a 1940's film noir movie. Tall and dark, she—through no fault or effort of her own—had the aura of a black widow spider, dangerous and ready to kill. In reality she was a perfectly nice person who was no more cruel or heartless than anyone else, but thanks to the effects of her long black hair, blood red lips, frosty blue eyes and taste for tight black skirts, her true personality was hidden by a false image of predatory delight. She had aroused the imaginations of the company's every male employee, Lloyd and Irwin included.

Even though the small talk she and Lloyd exchanged every morning was completely innocent, it still gave him the sensation of an illicit thrill. She was the first woman he had ever met with whom talking about the day's weather could

turn his cheeks red with both feelings of guilt and excitement. It was because of this strange reaction to her aura and
presence that he began to have some idea about how he was
going to get rid of Irwin.

The question that had given him the idea was that if he, an
attractive young man with a beautiful and someday-wealthy
young wife at home, was aroused by Anita's alluring attributes, then how would they affect a short, fat, balding man
who lived alone and who conceivably hadn't been out with a
woman in years? The answer to that question was obvious.

If he wanted to sabotage Irwin, he didn't have to ruin his
work, but his reputation. All he had to do was convince the
oaf that the sexy young receptionist was interested in him
and that he should take the initiative and start pursuing her.
The piggish man's advances would horrify Anita and she
would accuse him of sexual harassment, and if there was one
thing Mrs. McQueen had ever made clear to her board of
governors it was that this particular offence could be dealt
with in only one way. Irwin would be out of a job.

Lloyd became so excited by this idea that he, at first, neg-
lected to notice its one major flaw, but after his initial exhila-
ration died down it became immediately obvious. Exactly
how was he supposed to get Irwin to believe that Anita was
attracted to him? Any attempt at verbal communication was
out, because he never talked to Irwin outside business meet-
ings, so any kind of small talk would be immediately suspect.
He briefly thought about spreading a rumor through the
office, but he realized that this tactic could backfire if Anita
heard the news first and vigorously denied it.

He was working at his computer when the solution came
to him. He had just sent an email to a distributor when he

realized that he had just come upon the perfect way to communicate with Irwin. All he had to do was send him a few romantic emails anonymously and include enough clues in them for the poor fool to conclude that they were coming from Anita. Not only was it easy, but it would also be almost impossible for Irwin to trace the letters back to him after he was fired.

Trying hard not to giggle, he went to a Website and created a new email address for himself and used it to write the first love letter Irwin Curtis ever received in his 47 years of life.

> Dear Irwin,
> How I wish I were brave enough to approach you and say all of these things in person, but the thought of you rejecting me eye to eye is more than I can bear. Every time I see you walk past me I want to stand up and shout and have you look at me, but I stay quiet instead. Are you even aware of your power over me? Do you know how you make me feel? No matter what I do, I do it with you in mind. Just yesterday I bought a pair of turquoise earrings just because their color reminded me of that suit you always wear on Tuesdays. Maybe tomorrow I'll be brave enough to wear them to work and maybe you'll notice them and know who I am.
> With Love,
> Your Greatest Admirer

With a smile of cruel delight, Lloyd sent the email to Irwin with a simple click of his mouse. For the rest of the day he had to fight the urge to get up from his desk and go and see if it had had any visible effect on his target, but he managed to stay put. When five o'clock came and it was time to go home, he walked as casually as he could past Irwin's office. With the briefest possible of glances he caught a glimpse of Irwin sitting in his chair with an unusual smile on his face.

Instead of going directly home, like he usually did, Lloyd stopped off at a local shopping mall and walked into a small jewelry store.

"Hi, can I help you?" asked the smiling young woman behind the counter.

"Yes," he answered, "I'm looking for some turquoise earrings."

Ten minutes later he was back inside his car with a box of earrings in his pocket.

The next day he got to work a little earlier than usual and stopped to talk to Anita, who was already sitting at the front desk.

"Hi Lloyd." She smiled at him in that way she had that melted the male heart.

"Hi Anita," he smiled back. "How was your Thursday?"

"Pretty quiet," she admitted. "How was yours?"

"Not great," he lied, "me and Scarlet had a big fight."

"Really? That's too bad," she sympathized. "What was it about?"

"Something completely stupid. She can be so suspicious that whenever I try and do something nice, she has to question it."

"What do you mean?"

"Well, yesterday after work I decided it would be nice to just stop off at the mall and buy her a present. It wasn't her birthday or an anniversary or anything, I just thought it would be romantic to surprise her for no reason."

"That's sweet of you," Anita complimented him.

"She didn't think so."

"Why not?"

"Because she's so damn suspicious. She assumed I must have done something wrong if I got her a present for no reason. She accused me of cheating on her with another woman. Can you believe it?"

"That's horrible."

"I try and do something nice for her and she throws it in my face and turns it into this huge argument."

"What did you get her?"

"Just some earrings, nothing too fancy," he sighed, and wearily put his hands in his jacket pockets. "Oh," he muttered, "I have them right here." From out of his pocket he pulled out the box of earrings he had purchased the day before. "Stupid me, I threw away the receipt, so I can't even return them." He sighed again and turned to head towards his cubicle, when he stopped—as if he were struck by a sudden inspiration—and turned back to her. "Do you want them?" he asked her. He placed the box in front of her.

"Oh, I couldn't," she insisted unconvincingly.

"At least take a look at them," he suggested.

Cautiously she picked up the small box and opened it.

"They're gorgeous," she exclaimed.

"Take them, then," he prodded. "Otherwise I'm just going to throw them away."

She looked up at him, horrified.

"You wouldn't!"

"I can't return them and Scarlet refused to take them, so what else am I going to do with them?"

"Are you sure?"

"If you like them, they're yours."

"Thank you so much!"

"You're welcome," he shrugged. "At least this way I made someone happy."

With that he turned away from the desk and ambled down the hallway towards his cubicle. As he walked he turned his head unobtrusively and happily observed her replacing the earrings she had been wearing with the ones he had just given her.

As he got to his cubicle and started working, he tried not to dwell on the possibilities of what was happening at that very moment. Part of him feared that Irwin wouldn't even notice Anita's new earrings, or that he didn't even know what turquoise earrings looked like, but the other part of him buzzed nervously at the thought that Irwin had seen them and was at this moment convinced that the most beautiful woman in the office was his greatest admirer.

Despite his best efforts, he couldn't concentrate on his work, so he decided to push things even further by sending another email.

Dear Irwin,

I wore my new earrings today. Did you notice? If you did, then you know who I am. Every night I dream about you finding out. I dream that once you know who I am you will run to me after work and grab me and kiss me as passionately as any man has ever kissed a woman. Please, if you noticed and you know who I am, then could you make me the happiest woman in the world and make my dream a reality?

Dreaming of You Always,
Your Greatest Admirer

For a moment Lloyd actually hesitated before he clicked on send. He was about to set in motion a chain of events that could forever ruin a man's life, and just so he could get himself a nice office, a better paycheck and a more important job title. And was it even necessary in the first place? He was married to the owner's daughter. Surely that would be enough to make his ascent a certainty. But, as his finger hovered over his mouse's button, he convinced himself that nothing was assured. He and Scarlet could have problems and get divorced. The board members could try to halt his advancement to prove that they were not just Mrs. McQueen's puppets. Plus, even if his status in the family remained steady and the board heartily approved his moving up in the company, it could take years before he had an opportunity to advance. It was because of this that he finally brought down his finger, clicked the button and sent the email. In the business world the ambitious have to create their own opportunities, or else they just might waste their lives waiting for them to happen.

Lloyd couldn't sleep that night. He tossed and turned the whole eight hours, waking up Scarlet several times in the process. He felt like a small child waiting for Christmas morning, preoccupied by thoughts of what was inside the gift-wrapped boxes underneath the Christmas tree. But instead of imagining an exciting array of plastic action figures and remote controlled cars, he saw himself taking over Irwin's office and making it his own.

Despite the lack of sleep that night, Lloyd felt almost superhumanly energetic that morning. In his car he flew down the road, finding only the sweet glow of green at every traffic light, as if the universe was giving him a sign by clearing his way to work. When he got there, he felt his heart jump with anticipation at the sight of an empty front desk. Anita wasn't there. There had to be a reason for her absence, and he just hoped it wasn't the flu.

Lloyd kept his ears alert as he walked down the hallway to his cubicle, hoping to catch word of some hint that his plan had worked, but the office was silent. He got to his cubicle and waited. He couldn't get any work done, so he just sat there, impatiently anticipating some sort of intercom announcement, phone call or email.

Finally, just as the waiting was starting to make him feel ill, his phone rang at a quarter to 11. His hand trembled as he picked up the receiver and said hello. It was Mr. Kaufman. He wanted to see Lloyd right away. Still shaking, Lloyd hung up and walked over to the building's biggest office.

"Have you heard about what happened?" his boss asked him before Lloyd even had a chance to sit down.

"No," he admitted as he lowered himself into a chair.

"That idiot Curtis attacked Anita yesterday."

"You're kidding."

"Yeah, apparently someone sent him some mash notes and he thought they were from her. Can you believe that? How could he think a girl like that would be interested in a schmuck like him?"

"So what's going to happen to him?"

"He's gotta go," Kaufman shrugged. "You know how your mother-in-law feels about this sort of thing."

"How's Anita?"

"She's a little shaken up. I gave her the rest of the week off. We'll be lucky if she doesn't sue us. As it is, she's pressing charges against him."

"Really?" Lloyd hadn't even thought about that.

"You bet she is, and I don't blame her. We got it all on our security cameras. He just ran up to her and grabbed her and started kissing her. There's a word for that and people take it pretty seriously these days."

"So," Lloyd tried not to sound too eager, "what are you going to do about the opening this all creates?"

Kaufman smirked at this. Lloyd had failed in his attempt to not sound eager. It was obvious he wanted the job.

"The job's yours," he smiled. "Right from this moment on."

Half an hour later Lloyd had already moved everything from his cubicle into Irwin's office. Irwin hadn't even been allowed in the building that day, so Lloyd threw all of his leftover belongings into a box, with the exception of the notebook Irwin had used to keep track of his contacts and his schedule. Lloyd flipped through it and took note of all of the projects Irwin had been working on. He then turned on the computer in front of him and found all of the corresponding files. He wrote out their names and their locations on the hard drive, and then he turned the computer off and called the tech guy.

"Hi, Mike, it's Lloyd. They just moved me into Curtis' office and I need you to come over and wipe his drive for me. I've made a list of all the files I need you to save, and I want everything else to go."

Five minutes later Mike came over and took the computer away. He returned with it a half hour later and just like that,

Lloyd had managed to get rid of the only physical evidence—those two emails—that could have helped prove Irwin's alibi.

There was just one last loose end to tie up, and it required some delicacy on his part. He took a deep breath as he picked up his phone's receiver and dialed the number. His stomach started to flip flop as the other end started to ring.

"Hello," a woman answered, her voice tired and unsure.

"Anita?" he asked. "It's Lloyd. I just heard. Are you okay?"

"Oh, Hi Lloyd," she greeted him distractedly. "I'm fine, I guess. Just a little…y'know. I've never had anything like that happen to me before. I'm kinda shaken up."

"I don't blame you."

"Mr. Kaufman told me to take some time off, but I'm not sure that I want to. I don't want everyone to start thinking that I'm some kind of delicate flower."

"No one's going to think that," Lloyd reassured her. "I know that if any of us went through what you did, we would all be really disturbed by it."

"It really wasn't that disturbing," she insisted. "I mean it wasn't so much what he did, but the shock that he was doing it. He just came out of nowhere. The truth is I had him in a chokehold before he could do anything else."

"That's good."

"I've got four older brothers, so it wasn't the first time I've had to use it. I hate to admit this, but I almost felt sorry for him. He was so pathetic. He acted like he was surprised that I was so angry, as if he thought I had wanted him to do it."

"That's how these guys think, Anita," he explained to her. "They see an attractive young woman like you and they delude themselves into believing that you are somehow propositioning them. They're sick if you ask me."

"Yeah, you're right I guess."

"I heard you're pressing charges."

"The police want me to, but I'm not sure. He's already going to lose his job, I don't see what getting him arrested will do."

"It'll do two things, Anita. It might make sure he doesn't pull a stunt like this again, and it'll also send a message to the other guys who work here about what'll happen to them if they treat their female counterparts with such blatant disrespect."

"I never really thought about it like that," she admitted.

"Well, maybe you should."

"It's so nice to have someone like you to talk to," she complimented him.

"It's my pleasure."

"I suppose I should let you get back to work…"

Here is where it got tricky.

"Before you do, I have something I have to ask you. It's the worst possible time for me to ask it, I know, but I'm in real trouble here."

"What is it?"

"When I got home yesterday Scarlet apologized to me for being so suspicious about the earrings I bought her, and now she wants them. I told her I left them at the office to explain why I couldn't give them to her right away, but she's expecting me to give them to her tonight. I tried to buy another pair, but I couldn't find any that looked the same." He took a deep breath. "I hate to ask it, but could I have them back?"

"Of course, you can," she answered him.

"Are you sure?"

"Don't be ridiculous. I don't even want to wear them after what happened yesterday. According to the police, Mr.

Curtis claimed that those earrings were the reason he did what he did."

"I'm so sorry," he apologized.

"Why? You couldn't have known he would do something like that. Anyway, you bought them for Scarlet so they should go to Scarlet. It's only fair."

Lloyd felt incredibly relieved that Anita had been so understanding. She gave him her address and after work that night he drove to her apartment and picked up the earrings. Before he left he asked her just one thing.

"Would it be possible for you to keep this a secret? If Scarlet found out I gave these to you, I don't know what she would do."

"Don't worry about it," Anita reassured him. "I promise I won't tell a soul."

In the end it turned out that Lloyd really had lost the receipt for the earrings, so he decided that he might as well actually give them to Scarlet. Not used to receiving presents without a good reason, she became suspicious and accused him of having an affair. A fight soon followed, but Lloyd was too happy to acknowledge the irony.

• • •

For a while Lloyd worried about the fact that he felt no real guilt about what he had done to Irwin. Especially after Irwin died of a heart attack while sitting in the city lockup, waiting for his bail to be set. He wondered if maybe he was some kind of inhuman monster because his conscience didn't bother him more. He eased his mind by reminding himself of all the horrible things other businessmen had done that he had read about. His crime was—at worst—a minor misdemeanor in comparison. Plus, he figured he had nothing to do with the heart attack, which had more to do with genetics and Irwin's unhealthy diet than his legal troubles.

He was far more troubled by what he had done to Anita, who was devastated by the news of Irwin's death. She was convinced that she had killed him. She insisted that if she had followed her gut instinct and not pressed charges, then he would be alive today. No one could convince her otherwise. Not long after, her guilt caused her once-powerful aura to fade and her presence no longer enflamed the office's male imagination and she became just another receptionist.

But as the months passed, Lloyd worried less and less about his lack of guilt and eventually managed to almost forget about what he had done. Occasionally the memory of it would bubble up inside his head, but he could usually pop it as soon as it arrived. One afternoon, however, he had drunk far too much during a late lunch with Kevin and told him the whole story. Kevin seemed amused by the tale and promised not to tell anyone else. Lloyd wasn't sure he could trust him, but at this point it hardly mattered. Kaufman's gluten-free venture was a disaster, and it wouldn't be too long before the board decided he had to be replaced. Plus, his mother-in-law's health had been failing lately, which meant that it might not be too long before Scarlet owned the company, which—in essence—would mean that he owned the company, given Scarlet's distaste for the trivial concerns of business.

But unlike many in his position, who would feel invulnerable against any attempt at sabotage, Lloyd was acutely aware of how tenuous his position really was. Getting rid of Irwin had been so easy it proved to him that at no point should he get too comfortable where he was. Somehow someone had changed his report and he had to find out who it was before they could do any further damage to his reputation.

Right after Kevin returned to his office, Lloyd wrote out a list of all the people at the company who had a good reason to dislike him. He became a bit depressed by just how long the list was, because it took up a full page of single-spaced foolscap. He then went down the list and crossed out the names of all those who he felt weren't smart or devious enough to pull off a stunt like the one that had just been per-petrated on him. By the time he got to the end, every name had a line through it. As far as he was concerned there wasn't anybody at McQueen Comestibles who could have made the switch, but the fact that it happened was obvious proof that he was wrong. Somewhere working at the company was someone who was a lot smarter and more devious than he could ever imagine, and the only way he could think of to find out who this person was was to catch him or her in the act. It would require constant vigilance on his part, so much so that he found just the thought of it to be oppressively exhausting.

• • •

That night he waited until everybody else was gone before he left. He locked his office door behind him and walked slowly down the hallway, searching for anyone who might have also stayed late. Ahead of him he heard the sound of machinery whirring and clicking in the photocopy room, so he decided to investigate. The lights in the room were off, but the room was partly illuminated by the eerie florescent glow of the photocopier's laser. Standing in front of the copier was Anita. She heard him behind her and turned her head toward him. The soft light hit her face and

made her resemble a forlorn phantom straight out of a pulp novel.

"Hi Lloyd," she greeted him. "What are you doing here so late?"

"I was going to ask you the same thing."

She looked at the photocopier and hesitated before she explained herself.

"I needed to copy something for a friend, but I didn't want anyone to think I was stealing company supplies, so I waited until I thought everyone else had gone home," she admitted with a trace of guilt in her voice.

"Don't worry," he eased her mind. "I won't snitch. What is it that your friend needs?"

Anita paused once again.

"Justice," she finally answered.

"Excuse me?" asked Lloyd, assuming he had misheard.

"He's trying to get back at someone who wronged him. I'm helping him out."

"With photocopies?"

"With photocopies," she nodded.

Standing there, talking to Anita, Lloyd remembered how he used to feel when he exchanged small talk with her each morning, and that same intoxicating mixture of guilt and excitement surged through him and made him blush nervously. She looked incandescent and strangely serene standing in front of that copier, and he had never found her more beautiful.

"Well…" he tried to think of something to say to her, but he found himself so entranced by her presence he managed only a quivery "goodnight."

"Goodnight," she smiled at him before turning back to the photocopier.

Shaken, he slowly turned around and walked out of the room. He left the building and went home, where he was unable to explain to Scarlet why he was so quiet.

• • •

That night Lloyd had a dream. He dreamed that he was the star of an old black and white movie. He wore a fedora and talked quickly in short bursts of tough, hard-bitten dialogue. He looked handsomer than he did in real life, like a movie star and not a schmuck who worked in a Wichita-based bakery corporation. Everywhere he went was dark, and there seemed to be more shadows around than any kind of light. Around him he heard sharp, staccato melodies punctuating his every thought and movement.

He was in his office, but instead of a computer on his desk, there was a typewriter and bottle of scotch and a glass that had just been used. He could feel in his throat the burn of the alcohol as it went down. He poured himself another glass when his door opened and Anita walked inside. She too wore a hat, which consisted mainly of a wide round brim that covered her eyes. She wore a tight black dress that encased her body in such a way as to garner maximum attention. A cigarette burned between the fingers of her right hand, which—like the left—was covered with a long, black glove.

"We did it, kid," he said in greeting.

"Yes, we did," she agreed.

He motioned for her to sit in the chair in front of his desk, but she just shook her head. Even if she had wanted to sit down, her dress wouldn't have let her.

"Now that that fat pig is gone, it's just a quick trip to easy street," he smiled.

"What about Kaufman?" she asked.

Lloyd gulped his glass of scotch.

"Kaufman's finished," he told her. "He just doesn't know it yet. And once he's gone, you and I are going to take this company for everything it's worth."

"And what are you going to do about Scarlet and her mother?"

"I got those two so wrapped around my finger I could tell them it wasn't windy while we were standing in a hurricane and they'd believe me."

Anita smiled and took a long drag from her cigarette. She exhaled the smoke through her nostrils, and Lloyd's eyes fell upon the wispy tendrils as they rose up towards the ceiling. When he finally looked away from them, Anita was gone and he was sitting in front of Kaufman's desk.

"I know what you did," his boss sneered at him, "and you're a damn fool if you think I'm going to allow you to get away with it."

Lloyd smiled at this statement and watched as the older man lifted a cup of steaming hot coffee to his lips. He waited until Kaufman put the cup down before he answered him.

"And you're a damn fool if you think I'm going to let a decrepit old blowhard like you stop me," he sneered at the man.

"How dare you!" Kaufman stood up from his chair and exploded with anger. Immediately after the words came out, his face turned red and he clasped at his chest.

"W-w-hat—" he tried to speak as his heart made the first volley in what Lloyd knew would be a short and fatal attack.

Lloyd stood up and watched as Kaufman fell to his knees.

"It didn't have to be like this," he told his boss, "but you forced my hand. Now I'm going to wait a few seconds and then I'm going to run out of here and call for an ambulance, but I assure you, it isn't going to get here in time."

"Y-y-y-ou—" Kaufman sputtered at him helplessly, but before he could say anything else he slumped suddenly to the floor and lay as still as Lloyd had ever seen.

He turned to leave Kaufman's office, but instead of stepping out into the hallway, he found himself back inside his office.

Anita was there, in another dress. This one was red and somehow it was even tighter than the black one had been. They grabbed each other and began to kiss with the kind of passion that had little to do with love.

"The company's ours kiddo," he smiled when their lips finally parted.

She smiled back and kissed him again and that's where the dream ended.

• • •

When Lloyd woke that morning he felt almost giddy. He didn't know if it was imagining himself as some sort of '40s tough guy, the idea of getting rid of Kaufman or the thought of making out with Anita that made him feel more excited. For some reason he put a little more care into how he dressed and found himself whistling as he walked into work.

"You sound awfully cheerful today," Anita greeted him from behind her desk.

"What can I say," he smiled, "everything's coming up roses, kiddo."

"Excuse me?" she looked at him confused.

"Nothing," he grinned at her. "I'm just feeling good about my life." With that he began to walk towards his office, but he was stopped by the sudden rush of a spontaneous thought.

"Hey," he turned back towards Anita, "what are you doing for lunch today?"

"Sitting here, eating a salad," she answered him.

"Wanna grab something to eat? My treat."

"I don't know…" she hesitated, uncomfortable with the idea of going out with a married executive.

"It's not like that," he explained. "I just thought it might be nice to reward you for doing such a good job."

"That's very nice of you," she thanked him, "but it's not like what I do is really all that demanding."

"Don't be so self-deprecating," he smiled. "Come on, you can't say you don't deserve a nice expensive lunch."

She looked at him and thought about it.

"All right," she decided.

"Great! I'll see you at lunch."

"Okay."

• • •

"This is a nice place," admitted Anita as they sat down at a small table in the corner of a quiet Italian restaurant.

"Best pasta in Wichita," Lloyd smiled. "Which makes it sound worse than it actually is," he joked.

A young woman, obviously the owner's daughter, gave them their menus and asked them if they wanted anything to drink.

"I'm having some wine," announced Lloyd. "Do you want to share a bottle?"

"Should we? We still have to go back to work."

"Don't worry, we'll be fine. Which do you prefer, red or white?"

"I like red."

Lloyd scanned the restaurant's wine menu and picked out a red at random. He knew nothing about wine and was only ordering it to look more sophisticated.

The waitress left them to look over their menus and then came back with their wine and two glasses. They both ordered some pasta, and Lloyd took the bottle on their table and filled Anita's glass to the brim.

"That's a lot of wine," she laughed.

Lloyd shrugged playfully. "We only have an hour to get through the bottle," he explained.

He poured himself a less generous portion and took a sip from it before he leaned in and asked Anita to tell him about her life. Anita told him that she was born and raised in Wichita and that she had briefly moved to New York to try to become a model, but came back after a year.

"Why'd you do that?"

"I hated living in a city that big," she explained. "Plus," she blushed, "over there I wasn't anything special."

"What do you mean?"

"Well, in New York you can't cross the street without bumping into another model. There are so many beautiful women over there that unless you're truly extraordinary you're just a part of the background. Here in Wichita, I stand out. It's good for the ego."

"Better to be a big fish in a small pond," he mused.

"Exactly."

They continued chatting until their food arrived. While Anita began to eat, Lloyd poured her another glass of wine. The truth was that he honestly didn't know what his intentions were, but he felt certain that whatever they were the consumption of alcohol would make them easier to fulfill.

As they ate and talked, Lloyd stole long glances at Anita and found himself becoming more and more enthralled with her beauty with each look. The feeling both terrified and thrilled him at the same time. He knew he couldn't do anything about what he was feeling. If it got out he had an affair with the receptionist, both his career and his marriage would be ruined. But the longer he sat with Anita, the more he wondered if maybe those were sacrifices he would be willing to make.

A few minutes later they were finished. Lloyd paid the check and drove her back to the office. She was quiet during the ride, her skin showing just the slightest blush from the wine.

"How's your friend?" he asked, wanting to break the silence.

"Friend?"

"The one you were doing all that photocopying for yesterday. Is he any closer to getting that justice he was looking for?"

A small, satisfied smile fell upon her lips.

"A bit closer," she answered him.

"Well, I hope it turns out okay for him."

"It will," she nodded her head gently. "I'm sure it will."

• • •

Although Lloyd had deliberately drunk less wine than Anita, he was still feeling a bit tipsy when he walked into his office. He wasn't there for more than two seconds when Kevin popped his head through the door.

"Where have you been?" he asked Lloyd, his tone clearly indicating that something big just happened.

"I went out to lunch," answered Lloyd. "Why? What happened?"

"Kaufman came down here looking for you. I've never seen him look so angry. You're lucky you weren't here."

"What did I do?"

"He read the email you sent him."

"I didn't send him an email."

"Well, if you didn't, someone's been using your work account."

"I can't believe this."

"It gets worse," said Kevin.

"How?"

"Whoever wrote the email printed it out and left a copy on everyone's desk."

"Do you have a copy?" asked Lloyd.

"Yeah."

"Let me see it."

Kevin disappeared into his office and came back out with a sheet of paper in his hands. Lloyd took it from him and read it. Though the letter was short, it was long enough to potentially end his career.

Dear Fool,
I thought you might like to know that everyone who works at this company is counting the days to your retirement or—if we're very lucky—your early demise. We are tired of being victimized by your archaic ideas and idiotic business plans. If you had any real guts at all, you'd quit now or do us all a favor and jump out your window.
Yours Respectfully,
Lloyd Marlowe

As soon as he finished reading it, Lloyd ran past Kevin and down the hall to Kaufman's office. He rushed past the man's secretary and opened the door. Kaufman looked up from a report he was reading at his desk.

"I swear to God I didn't write this!" insisted Lloyd. "Someone used my computer when I wasn't in my office. I would never do this."

Kaufman looked almost unnaturally calm as he sat back in his chair.

"Close the door and sit down," he spoke quietly.

Lloyd did as he was asked and sat down in front of Kaufman's desk. For some reason, he felt himself overcome with a tremendous case of deja vu. Before he could figure out why, Kaufman handed him the red folder he had just been reading from.

"You're good with computers, aren't you Lloyd?"

"I swear I didn't send you that email, sir," Lloyd practically pleaded.

"And I suppose you also had nothing to do with what is in there."

Confused, Lloyd opened the folder and read what was in it. All he saw were rows of numbers that meant nothing to him.

"I know what you did," his boss sneered at him, "and you're a damn fool if you think I'm going to allow you to get away with it."

Lloyd almost jumped when he heard those words. He stared at his boss with a dumbfounded look on his face, until he noticed that there on Kaufman's desk was a full cup of steaming hot coffee. He knew what he had to do.

He sat back in his chair and threw the folder disdainfully onto Kaufman's desk and waited for the older man to take a sip. Almost as if on cue, Kaufman lifted the cup and put it to his lips.

"And you're a damn fool if you think I'm going to let a decrepit old blowhard like you stop me," he sneered at the man, relishing the opportunity to really say the words.

Again, as if on cue, Kaufman jumped up with rage and shouted "How dare you!" at Lloyd before his face suddenly turned red and he clasped at his chest. "W-w-hat—" he muttered pitifully while Lloyd watched him to fall to his knees. Even though he was stunned by what he was saying, Lloyd felt compelled to say the words he had spoken in his dream.

"It didn't have to be like this," he told his boss, "but you forced my hand. Now I'm going to wait a few seconds and then I'm going to run out of here and call for an ambulance, but I assure you, it isn't going to get here in time."

"Y-y-y-ou—" Kaufman tried to speak, but it was too late. His body slumped to the floor and stopped moving. Only then did Lloyd get up and run out of the office.

"Quick, call an ambulance!" he shouted. "Mr. Kaufman has had a heart attack!"

• • •

After the ambulance arrived to take Kaufman away, Lloyd used the confusion caused by the old man's coronary to steal the folder containing whatever it was that the old man thought could incriminate him. He shredded it, along with every copy he could find of the slanderous email that had been sent to Kaufman by whoever was trying to wreck his career.

He also had the tech guy change his office email account and protected it with several long passwords that he hoped would end any future attempts to pull the same trick twice.

Just before quitting time, word came back from the hospital. Kaufman was dead.

The funeral was held four days later. The day before, Lloyd was informed by the company's board and his mother-in-law that he was being promoted into the now-vacant position.

It should have been the happiest moment of his life, as it had been the climax he had been waiting for, but instead all he felt was an uncomfortable mix of paranoia and desire. Whoever was trying to bring him down was still out there and now that he was the boss they would undoubtedly double their efforts to get him fired. And he couldn't stop thinking about Anita. He realized that all his efforts had been meaningless when one day he found himself sitting in his new office and decided he would willingly give it all up for just one night with her.

His instincts told him to find a reason to fire her, but he couldn't bring himself to do it. Instead he did the worst thing he could do and made her his personal secretary. Not only did her closer proximity to him make him think about her that much more, but the move aroused the suspicions of his wife, who did not like the idea of her husband spending so much time with such a beautiful woman.

Another aspect of the new position he hadn't counted on was that his workload doubled. He worked 12 to 14 hours a day, and often didn't have time to eat lunch or take any kind of break. Most days he was the first person to arrive and the last to leave. One late night he found himself nodding off while trying to read a report describing how sales of the gluten-free cinnamon buns had recently gone on a shocking upswing, which meant that the product would start turning a profit in another two months.

Bleary eyed, he put down the report and opened up the bottom drawer on the right side of his desk. From it he pulled a large bottle of scotch and a clean glass. He poured himself a shot and gulped it down, grimacing as it burned his throat.

He sat back in his chair and heard a sound in the distance. He decided to investigate. He left his office and realized that the sound was coming from the copying room. He walked over to it and found Anita standing in front of the copier, looking glamorous and devastating in the stylish business suit she had worn to work that day.

"Still helping your friend out?" he asked her.

She flinched, surprised by the sound of his voice.

"Yes," she admitted as she turned towards him.

"He still seeking justice?"

"Yes."

"Is he any closer now than he was before?"

"Much closer. He's almost there."

"That's good to hear."

"Yes it is."

Lloyd started to turn away, but something stopped him. It was the same compulsion he had been fighting ever since that day he took Anita out for lunch. But this time he didn't feel like fighting it. Maybe it was the booze or the lack of sleep, but he no longer cared what could happen to him.

"Anita?" he spoke as he turned back towards her.

"Yes?"

"Are you doing anything tonight? I mean, besides making photocopies."

Her scandalously red lips turned upward into a knowing and willing smile.

"No, I'm not," she answered him.

. . .

Lloyd could literally feel his body tingle as he stepped into Anita's apartment. He found the danger inherent in this situation exhilarating. He was risking everything to be there and he hoped it was worth it.

"Would you like me to pour you a drink?" she asked him.

"Sure. What do you got?"

"I have some scotch. That's what you drink, right?"

"Yes it is."

"Neat or on the rocks?"

"Neat."

She nodded and disappeared into her kitchen and came back with a bottle and two glasses. She poured a drink for both of them, and they sat down on her black leather couch.

"I have to admit I've been waiting for you to get the nerve to ask me out," she told him as he took a sip from his glass.

"Really?"

"Hasn't it been obvious? I've been sending out so many signals."

Lloyd felt relieved hearing her say this. He had thought she had been indirectly propositioning him for the past few weeks, but he was afraid he had just been imagining it.

"This is good scotch," he said. For some reason he couldn't think of anything to say.

"Is it? My brother brought it over when I had the family over for Christmas."

"Well, he has good taste."

"I'll tell him that the next time I see him."

Lloyd looked around her apartment. It seemed different than it had been the last time he had been there to pick up the earrings.

"Did you redecorate in here?"

"Yes," she admitted.

Lloyd's eyes took in all the furniture and the artwork on the walls. As he studied them he couldn't help feeling that there was something out of place about them. It took him a minute before it occurred to him that there was no way Anita could have afforded to buy any of these items with her current salary as a secretary.

"Can I ask you something?" he turned towards her.

"Anything," she answered him.

"Did you make a lot of money as a model in New York?"

"I made almost nothing," she admitted. "I got a few jobs, but none of them paid very well."

"Are you currently seeing someone?"

"No, I'm completely unattached at the moment."

Lloyd frowned and stood up.

"Then how?" he asked with a sweeping gesture of his right arm, indicating the expensive furnishings.

"How what?" she played dumb.

"How did you afford all of this?"

She smiled and took a long sip from her scotch. Then she put her glass down on the table in front of her and sat farther back on her couch and spread her arms out across the back cushions.

"The company paid for all of it," she explained to him.

"What?"

"I got the money from the company."

"You mean you stole it?"

Her smile widened to reveal her perfect white teeth. Lloyd had seen that kind of smile before. It was the one people used when they were about to destroy you.

"No, you did," she told him.

"What?"

"You've been siphoning money out of the company's accounts for months now. Didn't you know?"

Lloyd stared at her, dumbfounded.

"You started doing it because you fell in love with me and wanted to impress me with expensive gifts," she continued. "I had asked you where you had gotten the money to pay for them and you told me you had inherited it from a rich uncle who had died."

Lloyd still could not speak as he tried to figure out what she was talking about.

"We've been having an affair for a while now," she explained. "It all started when you gave me those turquoise earrings."

"Are you insane?" he finally managed to say.

She just smiled.

"Unfortunately," she went on, "Mr. Kaufman found out about your embezzlement and tried to stop you, but you stopped him by putting a drug in his coffee that gave him a massive heart attack."

"You're insane!"

"Because of Kaufman's age and medical history, no one suspected that he had been murdered. Until today that is, when someone called the police and told them that evidence of your crime could be found in your office. They should be searching it right at this very moment."

Lloyd turned pale.

"Why?" he asked her. "Why are you doing this?"

Her smile vanished and she stood up from the couch.

"You made me think I killed a man!" she shouted at him.

"What?"

"He told me everything! I know what happened. You sent him those emails! You made him think I was in love with him. You gave me those earrings, knowing what he would do when he saw them! And when he died sitting in that prison cell you let me think it was my fault. That I was responsible!"

"How—"

"How do I know all this? I told you! He told me everything!"

"But he's dead!"

Without a word she turned away from him and walked into her room. A moment later she walked out again holding a large pile of photocopier paper.

"He was dead for two months the first time he contacted me," she told him. She held up a piece of paper from the pile. On it was a normal standard issue company memo, but in the middle of a paragraph about the past summer vacation schedule was a sentence that she had highlighted. It read: Lloyd pretended he was you. He told me you loved me.

"At first I thought it was a stupid prank," she explained, "but I kept getting messages like this on every photocopy I received. Like this one," she held up more photocopies, "and this one and this one. I checked other people's copies and they were normal. It took me a few weeks but I finally realized he was talking to me though the copying machine."

Hearing this, Lloyd flashed back instantly to the incident involving the report of his that had been mysteriously rewritten despite its never having left his hands. He had photocopied it. Feeling nauseous he stumbled into an expensive-looking chair.

"Gradually I learned exactly what had happened," she went on. "I can't believe you did that to me! It was Irwin's idea to get back at you. First he started toying with you by rewriting that report and then we came up with this plan to take away everything you had gotten from what you had done to us."

"But Kaufman! You murdered Kaufman!"

She shrugged.

"He really did find out about the missing money. The copier is connected to the phone line and Irwin had used the connection to get into the company's computers and move the money around into the various bank accounts we had taken out in your name. Kaufman noticed the discrepancies and we realized that sending you to death row to await a lethal injection would be the ultimate way to end our revenge."

Lloyd bent forward on the chair and held the back of his head with his hands.

"It really is neat how he can move around through the system like that," she said admiringly. "He wasn't very graceful when he was alive, but now that he's a ghost in the machine, little Irwin can really fly. Everything traces back to you. The case against you is airtight. And if any paperwork turns out to be missing during the investigation, I'm sure someone will eventually come across a helpful photocopy along the way."

"I can't breathe," Lloyd moaned.

"I don't doubt it."

She poured herself another glass of scotch and Lloyd tried to move out of the chair he was in, but he didn't have the strength to stand. They sat silently for a moment until the quiet was interrupted by the sound of Anita's apartment buzzer going off.

"That'll be the police," she explained. "I left a note in your office asking you to meet me here tonight."

She got up and opened the door. Two plainclothes detectives stood at the door and flashed her their badges.

"We're looking for a Lloyd Marlow," one of them said. "Is he here?"

• • •

No one would believe him when he said he was innocent. The case against him was open and shut with a paper trail that was a mile long. At the trial Kevin testified about what Lloyd had done to Irwin, and Anita was a very credible witness who the prosecution was able to successfully present to the jury as a poor pawn in one man's sick quest for wealth and power. Reams of photocopies were admitted into evidence, along with the bottle of drugs that had been found in his desk. The jury deliberated for less than hour before they returned with a verdict. He was guilty on all counts, the most serious of which was first degree murder. The judge, a conservative man not known for his leniency, sentenced Lloyd to death. Lloyd screamed out in protest in the court, insisting that he had not murdered David Kaufman. The guards tried to get him to calm down, but he would not stop. Even after they had jolted him with a taser, he still kept on shouting.

Scarlet was not there to see it. Their divorce had already been finalized three months earlier, just a week before her mother died from a sudden stroke. The company was now hers, and, no longer able to trust anyone else to take care of it, she took over the position that both Kaufman and her ex-husband had held. But because she lacked experience, she promoted Kevin and made him her equal in the decision-making process.

Anita quit her job at McQueen Comestibles. Her expensive furniture was seized as evidence for the trial against Lloyd, but that didn't matter, because she had access to several Swiss bank accounts that the prosecutors had not found in the course of their investigation. With that money she decided to move back to New York, having decided that perhaps it was better to be a small fish in a big pond after all.

The Girl in the Water

THOUGH THE GROUND WAS COLD, she wore no shoes and the frozen grass cut sharply into her feet. She stood at the edge of the small pond, whose water would be frozen in only a few days, and she pondered the beauty of her own reflection.

It is this which has brought me here, she thought to herself. *If I had been born something other than fair, things would have been different.* She lifted a pebble from the ground, threw it into the water and watched as her beauty rippled and waved in front of her. *Or,* she admitted, *they would have been exactly the same.*

She knelt down and dipped her hand into the water. It hurt to touch it. It was so cold. She did not know if she could do it. She was afraid. They thought her mad—and maybe she was—but she was not so mad that a decision such as this could be so easily made.

What if there is nothing after this? she wondered. *Or what if there is and it is a place of eternal torment where I shall suffer forever for my self-sacrifice? What if I am mad? What if what I have seen were the visions of a poor sad girl who has lost her father and whose grief has turned her mind against her? What if I do this and nothing happens?*

She had no answers for any of these questions. She looked up and saw that the sun was beginning to rise.

She closed her eyes and stepped into the water. It hurt so much, but she did it again with her other foot. Slowly she walked forward, the cold water rising higher and higher with each step, until it surrounded her and she could no longer breathe. A calmness fell over her, and she waited. It

didn't take long and when it was over, all her questions had been answered.

. . .

Her brother was leaving the castle to go back to school. He had come back to attend the king's funeral and the new king's coronation and marriage. He did not like being there. He hated the gossip and constant intrigue that were so vital to living a healthy life in court. Their father was the learned expert of this game, having long sacrificed his pride to master the art of flattery and sycophantic adoration. Her brother hated their father, but she loved him. She knew he was a fool and knew that if she knew it, it could be a secret to no one else, but she loved him all the same. He alone had raised her since her mother died, and in that time had shown her only the greatest affection and had done all he could to ensure that her life was happy and secure. Unlike her brother, who was appalled whenever their father trod upon his own dignity to earn the admiration of the king and queen, she recognized that he suffered these humiliations not for the sake of his own aggrandizement, but so that his children would prosper. It was for this reason that she had long ago decided that he had earned her undying loyalty, even when his wishes ran counter to her own desires.

His belongings packed and his horse ready, her brother was set to leave, but he wanted to talk to her before he left. He had found a letter in her room, and its contents worried him.

"The prince writes that he loves you," he said to her, "and I can believe that—for the moment—his feelings are genuine, but," he placed her hand into his, "I do not think it would be wise for you to encourage his affection."

She stayed silent and he went on, explaining why he felt she should not be swayed by the prince's romantic entreaties.

"His will is not his own," he told her. "He is subject to his birth and this does not allow him to choose his fortune the same way unvalued persons do. He cannot allow himself to follow his heart when his heart knows so little about the health and safety of the state. He must listen to the demands of his practical mind, even if it means sacrificing that which he truly loves."

She lowered her head. She knew that what he was saying was true.

"So though he sends you loving letters and dear kindnesses, remember that he cannot be trusted to keep the promises his gifts imply. I am afraid that his words, as bewitching as they can be, might trick you into giving him the gift of your virtue, a gift that—once given—cannot be taken back. For the sake of the honor of our name do not let yourself be moved by his pretty words and trinkets into surrendering that which so many fair young girls forever regret the impetuous loss of."

She looked back up at him.

"I'll do as you ask," she told him, "and do my best to politely decline the advances of our prince, but," she smiled wickedly, "in return I'll ask that you do not play the hypocrite and use pretty words and trinkets to capture from other young maidens that which you have just bade me to hold dear and protect."

Her brother smiled at this.

"Do not worry—" he began before he was interrupted by the sound of approaching footsteps. A voice called out to them. It was their father. "I stayed too long," her brother sighed.

"Still here, my son?" their father laughed. "Go! You have my blessing, as long as you remember that which I have taught you. Do you remember? Stay quiet and be not rash. Be familiar, but not vulgar. Do not get into fights, but let every man know that you will battle them if they push you in that direction. Listen, but do not speak. Be judged, but do not judge others. Allow others to know that you are noble by your manner, not your wealth. Dress well. Lend money only if you are willing to lose that which you have lent and the friend you have lent it to. Borrow only if you are willing to be thought of as less than a man. And most importantly, be yourself. Now, farewell, you have my blessing to go."

Her brother, who had managed to make it through the entirety of their father's speech without once rolling his eyes heavenward, nodded.

"With your blessing, then, I shall go."

"Go! Go!" their father hugged him.

When the embrace ended, her brother turned to her and spoke one last time.

"Good-bye, my sister. Remember well what I have said to you."

"I will," she promised.

He nodded at this and turned away and left them.

"What did he say to you?" asked her father.

"It was about the prince," she told him.

"Ah," her father sighed. "I have noticed that he has recently taken to giving private time to you."

"Yes, he has."

"And is it because of this that your brother has spoken to you?"

"Yes."

"Why? What has the prince done that your brother should think to comment on it?"

She paused for a moment, but she had never been the type of girl to keep secrets.

"The prince has—of late—made clear his affection for me."

"Affection? You speak like a green girl! There is another word for it, but you are too innocent to let it be heard by your ears. I warn you, the risks of returning his 'affection' are more than you are prepared to handle."

"His affection seems honorable," she protested softly. "When he speaks to me, it almost sounds as if he is praying."

"And I am certain what he is praying for," her father answered her. "No good can come from this. From this moment on you are to ignore the prince's affections and avoid him as best as you can. Do not be rude or disrespectful, but—for the sake of our name—do not put yourself in a situation where his actions may result in our slander."

While some daughters may have been angered by an order such as this, she was not one of them.

"Yes, sir," she answered him sincerely.

From that moment on she would do her best to avoid the prince.

• • •

It was a dark night. Not a single star shone to break through the blackness, and the moon above was only a tiny sliver in the sky. Thunder and lightning roared and flashed as storm clouds formed and let loose a torrent of rain. She sat alone in her room, working on a small tapestry that was to be a gift to her brother when he returned from school during the summer. The castle was still, and were it not for the thunder, the silence would have been heavy and absolute. To keep her mind as busy as her fingers, she hummed the simple tune her mother had always sung when she did her sewing. She did it almost unconsciously and when she became aware of it, she felt sad that it had been so long since she had thought of her mother.

She had been just a child when her mother died, her brother not that much older. Over the years it was becoming harder and harder for her to summon up memories of the woman, so she was usually overcome with grief whenever one happened accidentally into her mind.

A bright blast of lightning exploded just outside her window, followed quickly by a loud clap of thunder. The combination had taken her by surprise and caused her heart to race and her pulse to quicken. She had dropped her sewing, and she bent forward to pick it up when a powerful wind burst through her window and threw her to the floor. The flames of her candle were extinguished, and the room became pitch black.

The storm outside roared angrily at the world and its cries became deafening. She tried to stand but the wind would not let her. She covered her ears and trembled on the floor, growing more and more afraid with each passing second. Fear and panic combined in her to such a degree that she was a second away from screaming aloud when—as if it had been commanded—the storm outside stopped and the wind ceased. There was now only silence and darkness. Still trembling, she stood up uneasily and went to her candles so she could regain the light, but she stopped when she saw the faint glow that hovered at the edge of her door. Slowly, as she stared at it, the glow grew brighter and turned a deep emerald green.

It shaped itself from a chaotic swirling mass of vapors into the silhouette of a small, beautiful woman.

It was all she could do to stand there and behold it. The process took seconds, but her shock stretched them into an infinity of days. At the end of it, a being who exactly resembled the last memory she had of her mother stood before her.

She tried to say something, but no words would come.

Hush, she heard her mother's voice echo inside her head, *there is no need for you to speak, as I have not ears to hear your words, though—I must admit—the sound of them would delight me more than they could ever say. As it is, all you have to do is think of what you want to say and I will know how to answer you. Do you understand?*

Yes, she answered in her head.

Do you know who I am? asked the spirit.

You look like my mother, just before she died, she answered.

Then you do remember me, the spirit smiled. *I was certain that you had forgotten. It has been so long and you were so young when I left.*

I remember.

Tears began to fall down her cheeks.

Why do you cry? asked the spirit. *Are you not happy to see me?*

I am happy, she nodded, *I just never thought I would ever see you again. You are as beautiful as you were in my memories. I never knew if they were real or just the fantasies of a foolish young girl.*

Her mother's spirit paused for a moment, as she allowed herself to look at her daughter's memories. The smile on her face deepened as each second passed.

They are real, the spirit shimmered, *and I can feel the love in them. It makes me wish things had been different.*

Me too, she agreed.

But then if I had lived I would not be able to appear to you now and warn you of what is to come, the spirit admitted. *For that is why I am here. I wish it were just to see you once again, but the powers that govern us would never permit me to come back for such a trivial reason. No, I had to wait until this moment, when you are about to make a decision that will affect not only you, but your family and the entire kingdom as well.*

How so? she asked.

You have been ordered by your father—my husband—to refuse the entreaties of the prince of this land. Listen to me now. If you do as your father asks, then he will die. And so will your brother. And the prince. And the king and the queen and a host of others you have never met.

How can you know this?

I have seen it. The powers that govern us have shown it to me. The prince nears a kind of madness. His torment has been deepened by a devil who poses as the ghost of his father. You are the only person who can keep him sane, but if you do as your father tells you, then all will be lost. No one will survive.

No, she shook her head, *I do not believe you.*

It is the truth, the spirit insisted.

No, you speak of devils and that is what I think you are. You are a demon who has stolen the memory of my mother and used it to convince me to defy my father, knowing it will lead us to ruin.

No, that is not true. Listen, child—

No! I will not listen. Leave me! Go back to your foul hell and do not come back! I will not be swayed by your resemblance to a woman I barely knew to disobey the man who I love above any other.

But my daughter—

Be gone!

The room exploded in a flash of blinding light. She fell to the ground and lay there still for what felt like a passing moment. Slowly her eyes opened and her head ached. Light from the morning sun broke through her window and felt warm against her face. It was then she realized that she had been asleep.

"It was not real," she told herself. "It was just a dream."

It took her some time, but eventually she was able to rise from the ground. She picked up her sewing and tried to remember what she had just gone through in her unconscious mind, but already the memory of it was fading. After a few minutes all she could remember was that the dream had been about her mother.

• • •

As the days passed, she avoided all contact with the prince. During that time he had slipped several notes under her door, but she did not read them. She wanted to because the prince had a poet's gift for the language and his words were often capable of moving her to tears, but she obeyed her father and left them unopened in a pile in her room.

By now she had completely forgotten about her dream, and she felt certain that she was doing only good by listening to her father. That is until, one morning, she was visited by the prince.

She had been in her room, working on her brother's tapestry, when she heard the sound of her door slowly opening. She looked up and watched as the prince entered. She had never seen him look so pathetic. His clothes hung on his body as if they were distant afterthoughts, thrown on only to deny others a view of his naked self. He shivered in front of her, trembling as if he had just seen the violent end of all he had ever loved. She tried to say something, but there was nothing to say, so she just sat with her sewing in her hands as he approached her. When he reached her, he grabbed her by her wrist and held it as hard as he could. It hurt, but she made no sound. He sank down to his knees and—with her wrist still in his hand—fell back an arm's length away. From this distance he stared at her, as though he were an artist readying to paint her portrait. He stayed still for a long time. Then he started to tremble, shaking her arm as he held it. He nodded slowly three times and from somewhere inside of him came a sigh so piteous and profound it felt as though it could shatter him if it continued a moment too long. Then he let her go and got up and walked towards her door, never taking his eyes off her.

Though she had stayed calm while he was there, once he was gone she began to panic.

What have I done? she asked herself.

Before she could answer her own question, she felt herself rise from her chair and run out of her room to find her father.

He would know what to do.

• • •

After she had gone to her father, he had asked for the letters the prince had given her and she had handed them over to him. An hour later she was walking towards her room when she heard her father reading one of them aloud in the castle's lobby.

" 'I am ill at these numbers. I have not art to reckon my groans. But that I love thee best, O most best, believe it.

Adieu. Thine evermore, most dear lady, whilst this machine is to him,' " her father paused before adding "and he ends it here with his signature."

Without being seen she crept into the lobby and saw that he had been reading the letter to both the king and queen. Wanting to hear more, she hid behind a curtain and listened as the three of them discussed this worrying situation.

"And how has she received this love?" asked the king.

"What do you think of me?" asked her father, answering a question with a question.

"I think you are a good and honorable man," answered the king.

"I am glad to hear it, but would you think me thus if I had—knowing of the prince's true feelings—allowed my daughter to receive them as she would the affection of any other man? Could you not then accuse me of attempting to move beyond my rank by encouraging a union between our families? I would not have that, so when my daughter came to me and told me of our good prince's actions I did what I felt I must as a good servant to you. I ordered her to deny him her favor and accept no more of his gifts, and it is here where I am afraid I have erred. For I fear that it is this rejection that is the cause of the prince's strange behavior. It is his love for my daughter that has sent him into the madness which we all now mourn."

"Do you think this is true?" the king asked the queen.

"It may be," she answered him.

"Is there any way for us to know for sure?" the king asked her father.

"I think there is. You know how he has taken to walking this lobby for hours each night?"

"Yes," answered the king.

"At such a time I shall send over my daughter to speak to him. I will tell her to return to him the last of his letters. If I am correct and he does love her, an action such as this should provoke him to act out in either anger or sorrow. We both shall watch, hidden behind that curtain"—she nearly jumped when she realized he was referring to the curtain she was at that moment hiding behind—"and mark the encounter as it unfolds."

The king nodded.

"That is what we shall do," he agreed.

Knowing that she may soon be called upon by her father, she quietly, but quickly, removed herself from behind the curtain and ran to her room. She sat there with her sewing for a good hour before her father appeared at her door with the king at his side.

• • •

There was something about the new king that made her uncomfortable. This had been true even before his recent coronation, back when he was just the king's brother and the prince's uncle. It had something to do with his eyes. They were cold and unforgiving, even when he was smiling and laughing. They were not his brother's eyes, which were the brightest and bluest she had ever seen.

The former king's death had shocked her greatly. The prince's father had been the strongest and the healthiest man she had ever known. She had loved him as all those around him had loved him. He had been their protector, and his every decision made it clear that he would have willingly risked his soul if it meant saving any one of them from the fires of hell. This was not true of the new king, who—despite his resemblance to his brother—looked as though he would damn everyone before him if it meant avoiding his own judgment for even a second longer.

But what had shocked her even more than the death of their king was their queen's decision to marry his brother just a month after he was taken. It seemed to her a union that went against all manner of decency, but she never said a word to anyone about her disapproval. This silence was partly because she knew it was not her place to make such judgments and that no one was interested in the thoughts of a silly young girl. But she kept quiet mostly because with the rise of the new king, her father's prominence rose as well. He was now the king's closest advisor, which made him the second-most powerful man in the country. There had been others more deserving of such a role, but all of them had questioned the king's decision to marry his sister-in-law and they had all been punished for speaking out against it. Her father alone had been ambitious enough to bite his tongue and do nothing but congratulate the king for taking such a wonderful woman as his bride, and his reward was the highest position in the kingdom a common man could ever hope to achieve.

So to speak out against the king would mean speaking out against her father, an action she would never willingly take.

She joined the two men and walked with them towards the lobby. As they walked the king explained to her what they wanted her to do, and she pretended that she was hearing their plan for the first time. Along the way they were joined by the queen and two odd and obsequious young men she had never met before.

Apparently, they were friends of the prince, and they reported to the king and queen that to their eyes and ears he was acting normally. They also mentioned that a group of actors had arrived at the castle and that the prince had greeted them warmly and was looking forward to the performance they were going to give later that night. The king thanked them for their information and asked them to help the actors any way they could if it meant keeping the prince's spirits up. After that the two men left and the king asked the queen to leave as well.

"My dear girl," the older woman said before she left, "I do hope that it is your beauty which is the happy cause of my son's wildness, and that your virtues shall be enough to cure him of his madness."

"I hope so too," she agreed as her eyes looked down at the floor below.

With that the queen left.

As they waited for the prince to come, her father handed her a book and the letters she had given him earlier that day.

"Pretend you are reading this before you approach him," he told her, "that way he will not suspect that your meeting was not by chance."

The sound of footsteps echoed through the lobby.

"Here he comes," said her father to the king. "Let us hide before he sees us."

The two men ran and hid behind the curtain to their right, and the prince entered the lobby. He looked very sad and depressed and was talking to himself. She lifted up her book and pretended to read it, but he was too preoccupied by his thoughts to notice her. She strained her ears to hear what he was whispering, but she caught only a few words here and there. From them she gathered that he was talking about the world beyond the mortal realm, but that was all.

A few minutes passed until finally he looked up and noticed her. He spoke to her and she greeted him back.

"Hello, my lord," she closed her book. "How are you today?"

"Well," he nodded casually, "well," he repeated, "well."

She had never seen him look so defeated. She wanted to grab him and give him a hug, but instead she did as her father wanted and gave him what amounted to a slap in the face instead.

"My lord," she swallowed, her words sticking in her throat, "I have remembrances of yours that I have long wanted to redeliver." She held out the letters he had written to her. "Please take them."

The silence that followed lasted only seconds, but she feared it would never end.

He looked at her as though she had just unsheathed a long dagger and plunged it deeply into his heart.

"Those are not from me," he insisted coldly. "I never gave you ought."

"My honored lord, you know they are from you. You know of the words that fill them and I ask you to please take them back."

He stared at her. He made every attempt to look calm, but she could see the anger in his eyes.

"Are you chaste?" he asked her.

"My lord?"

"Are you fair?"

"I don't understand."

"If you are chaste and fair, your chastity would not deign to acknowledge your beauty."

She had no idea what he was saying, but she tried to answer him as best she could.

"Does a person's beauty not get along with their chastity?" she asked him.

"Yes," he agreed. "For it is easier for the power of beauty to undo chastity than it is for chastity to make things beautiful."

She stood there and tried to figure out what this had to do with her giving him back her letters. Before she could find an answer, he spoke once again.

"I did love you once," he admitted.

"Yes, I know, my lord. You said so in your letters."

"You should not have believed me!" he shouted at her. "I loved you not!"

She looked down at the floor, unable to bear his humiliation.

"Then I was fooled by your deception," she answered softly.

He grabbed her roughly by her shoulders. She dropped her book and the letters spilled out onto the floor. He stepped on them as he twirled her around and threw her to the ground.

"Get yourself to a convent!" he ordered her. "Would you spend your life as a breeder of sinners? I myself have committed such crimes that it would have been better if I had not been born! I have more offenses in my past than I have days that I have lived! What good is a world full of men like me?"

Before she could answer him, he shouted at her again. "Go!" Tears were beginning to stream down his face. With the back of his sleeve, he wiped them away.

At this she herself began to weep. There was no question now. Her rejection had driven the prince mad.

"Heaven help him," she prayed in a whisper.

Before her prayer could be heard, the prince turned around suddenly and bent down and grabbed her again.

"If you do marry, take this plague as your dowry; be as chaste as ice—as pure of snow—and you shall still end up slandered. Go to a convent!" He let her go and started to walk away before he turned back and grabbed her again. "Or if you marry, marry a fool! Wise men know what monsters you women make of them! Go!"

She prayed aloud once again, but he ignored her and continued ranting.

"I know how your kind paint your faces. You have been given one face, yet you insist on making another! You tease and laugh and dance, and I will have nothing more to do with it! It has made me mad and I say we shall have no more marriage!" He turned to her one last time. "To a convent, go!" he shouted before he disappeared out of sight.

She sat on the floor of the lobby and wiped away her tears, though they still flowed ceaselessly from her eyes.

What have I done? she asked herself again. *He was a good man and I have turned him into a wretched lunatic.*

The king and her father appeared from behind the curtain and ran to her.

"That was not love!" the king insisted as her father helped her up. "But," he decided, "I also do not think it was madness."

She was confused by the king's judgment. *If that was not madness, then what was?*

"It is as if there is a darkness in his soul," the king continued, "and I am afraid I must send him away before that darkness consumes him. He shall go to England." He turned towards her father. "What do you think?"

"Before you send him away, you should let the queen talk to him. I will listen to their conversation and if it proves that you are right, then I agree that he should be sent to England or wherever else you think it best."

The king nodded and together they left the lobby.

Her father took her back to her room, and she went in and lay down on her bed and cried until it was time to get ready for dinner and the prince's play.

· · ·

In all her days as a member of the court, she could think of no other dinner in which she was so uncomfortable. The prince was there and he kept looking over at her, but it was obvious that the majority of his attention was focused on the king and queen. Whenever he looked over at the king, a horrible smile descended upon his face. It unnerved her greatly to look at it, but then—after what had happened in the castle's lobby just a few short hours ago—everything he did made her feel that way. She had pitied him before, but now she feared him. When a normal person went mad, the result could be frightening, but when the sickness invaded the thoughts of a truly great man, like the prince, then it could mean the beginning of an apocalypse. Knowing that he was to be sent to England didn't ease her fear any. She knew that as long as he was alive, she could never truly feel safe again.

Before they were finished, he disappeared from the table to talk to the actors who were performing that night. She felt no relief when he was gone, knowing she would soon see him again. A few minutes later, the king bade them rise and everyone followed him out of the dining hall to the lobby, where a stage had been set. Chairs had been placed in front of it and after the king and queen sat down, she chose one close to them.

The prince was already there and spoke to the king and her father with words of sarcastic mockery that everyone tried their best to ignore. The queen asked him to sit beside her, but he refused.

"No, mother," he smiled, "I am attracted elsewhere."

He walked over to her and knelt down to speak to her.

"Lady," he asked her, "should I lie in your lap?"

She tried not to look at him as she spoke.

"No, my lord," she said.

He smiled and laid his head upon her lap.

"I meant like this," he explained.

"I misunderstood, my lord."

"You did?" he asked as he lifted his head back up. "What do you think I mean?"

"I thought nothing, my lord."

"That's a fair thought," he decided.

"What is, my lord?"

"Nothing," he mocked her.

She wanted to slap him. He was so close and it would have felt so good, but as mad and hateful as he was, he was still the prince and there was nothing she could do but withstand his abuse.

"You are merry, my lord," she told him through gritted teeth.

"Am I?"

"Yes, my lord."

He stood up and stretched out his arms dramatically.

"Well, what should a man do but be merry?" he asked her.

She stayed quiet. He smiled and turned and looked over to his mother, the queen.

"For look how cheerful my mother looks and my father died only two hours ago!"

"No, my lord," she corrected him, "it has been two months since your father died."

He turned back to her and laughed.

"So long? Then it is amazing he hasn't been already forgotten! Two months! Then there's hope a great man's memory might outlive his life half a year!"

The play started, but she was too preoccupied by the prince to give it any notice. The actors played out a strange pantomime and left the stage before they returned and began to speak aloud. As they talked the prince watched with rapt attention, looking every now and then over his shoulder to see the reactions of his mother and the king.

She looked at him and for the first time in two months saw a glimmer of the man she had once known as the prince. She looked into his eyes and knew then what she should have known all along. He, like the actors on the stage, was performing and she and the others were the unwitting cast members of his play. He was not mad. Every word and movement, as senseless as they had seemed, had been a deliberate act to lead them to this moment here. But why? For what purpose did he cause them so much misery?

She turned and looked back at the stage. An actor was speaking, but she was too immersed in her own thoughts to make out what he was saying. She watched as he knelt down beside another actor who was lying in a false sleep on a bench and lifted a vial from his cloak. He uncorked it and poured its contents into the sleeping man's ear.

The prince stood up and shouted.

"The serpent poisons Gonzago in his own garden!" He then turned and directly faced the king. "And you shall now see how the murderer marries the king's wife!"

She looked over to the king and was shocked by the look of horror on the man's face. His color was ashen, and he shook as though he had seen the very worst part of his damnation. He stood up suddenly and lurched past the people around him.

"Are you all right, my lord?" asked the queen.

Her father stood up and announced to everyone that the play was over.

"Give me some light," gasped the king as he stumbled towards the room's exit.

Her father shouted for light as everyone followed the king out of the lobby.

She looked over at the prince. He looked as happy as a weasel who had just successfully stolen a hatchling's egg.

Whatever it was he was doing, he has done it, she thought to herself as she got up and followed the others out of the lobby.

• • •

Having had enough of the court's high intrigue, she decided to return to her room and go to bed. She was very tired and sleep came to her within a few minutes. She lay in a warm, comfortable state until a noise from within her room woke her. She sat up and saw, illuminated from the moonlight through her window, her father standing beside her.

"What is it, father?" she asked him sleepily.

He did not answer her. Instead he bent over and gave her a kiss on the cheek. His lips were strangely cold, and she found the gesture unsettling. She rose from her bed, but before she could ask him why he had kissed her, a knock came from her door. Her father turned away from her and before she could say a word, he faded away as if he were an ethereal spirit.

Another knock came from the door. Her eyes opened and she found herself lying in her bed. She had been dreaming about her father, but the knocks were real. Slowly, she got up and wrapped a blanket around her shoulders and opened the door.

It was the queen. She looked dazed. Her skin was pale white, and her hands trembled.

"What is it, my queen?" she asked. "What could be so important that you of all people would visit me at so late an hour?"

"My poor girl," the queen lamented, "I cannot bear to tell you, but I would not have the news given to you by anyone else. It is my burden, for he is my son and for that I am at least part responsible for his crime."

She felt her skin tingle and the hairs on her body rise. She knew what news the queen was to deliver. Somehow she knew, but she refused to weep until she heard the words.

"Your father," the queen wept, "is dead. My son has murdered him in my room. He caught him listening to us from behind a curtain and slaughtered him with his blade."

She had now heard the words, and she began to weep.

• • •

She took little notice as the days passed by her. Her father was buried and the prince, his murderer, was sent to England. She stayed quiet and worked on her sewing. She spoke to no one and ate very little. Everyone decided it was best to leave her alone to grieve.

As he had done the night of his murder, her father continued to appear to her in her dreams. Each time he did, it seemed as though he was attempting to speak to her, but he could not manage to get the words out of his mouth. She would awake from these dreams sad and frustrated, wishing for just one more chance to speak to her father.

It had been three weeks since his death, and she was becoming weak. She had no appetite and could not bear the thought of food, but her body did not share her aversion and was beginning to shut down out of anger. It was only noon, but she could barely keep her eyes open as she sat in her room with her almost-finished tapestry. Unable to hold out for a second longer, her body gave up and she fell from her chair to the floor. She did not feel the impact, because her consciousness had left her and she was no longer physically aware.

She lay there long enough for the sun to set before something was able to rouse her out of her faint and get her to open her eyes. It was the sound of her father's voice.

"Get up, my daughter," he said to her.

Her eyes opened and she looked up at him. He looked the same as he had in her dreams.

She began to cry.

"What is the matter, my girl? What reason have you for tears?"

She wiped them away as she sat up on the floor.

"This is just another dream," she answered him. "For a moment I thought you were real."

He smiled at her.

"Then dry your eyes, because this is not a dream. I am here, returned from the place where spirits dwell, to talk to you about a matter of much importance."

"What?" she asked as she stood up and faced him. Standing there it did feel to her that if this was a dream, it felt far more real than any she had ever experienced before.

"Do you even have to ask?"

"Your murder?"

"That is right. My foul and cruel murder at the hands of that spoiled and wretched boy."

"What can there be to talk about? You are dead and he is gone to England."

"He is gone, but he will be return," answered her father's ghost.

"How do you know?"

"It is a gift given to the dead. Having suffered in the past, we are allowed to see what happens in the future."

"What happens?"

"That, my fair and honest daughter, depends on you."

"How?"

"Before I tell you, let me ask you a question. Do you love the prince?"

"Of course not! How could I love the man who murdered you?"

"Did you love him?"

She paused before she spoke.

"Yes," she finally admitted. "I was so moved by the words in his letters that I did love him once, but that was before you told me I was to no longer accept his affections."

"Were you so moved that the memory of your love could keep you from seeking out the justice the murderous fiend deserves?"

"No, of course not. He no longer even seems a man to me. I think of him as a treacherous animal, whose death I would no more mourn than that of the pig or cow served on my plate."

"Good," her father smiled.

• • •

The first thing she did after her father's spirit left her was get something to eat. She needed her strength. As she ate, she went over in her mind everything he had said to her.

"Do as the prince did and pretend that you are mad," he had ordered as he explained to her what she had to do to take revenge against not only the prince, but all those who allowed his murder to happen. "So that they will more easily accept and understand that which is to follow."

That wouldn't be too hard. Her recent grief had been so severe many in the court already feared that her sanity had been affected by it. She tried out her act around the castle and within a few days got to give it its first real test when she took it to the queen.

"Where is the beauteous majesty of this land?" she asked aloud, even though she could see the queen standing just a few feet in front of her.

"How are you, my lady?" the queen asked.

At this she started to sing. Everyone in the room stared at her with looks of pity. The song she sang suggested that she was more sad about the prince being gone than the death of her own father. The king entered the room, and he too looked stricken as she sang. He asked her a question and she answered him with nonsense.

When she left them, they looked heartbroken, saddened by the belief that lunacy had taken hold of her mind. As she walked away she allowed herself a small smile, knowing how their sympathy for her only made their anger towards the prince grow.

They sent someone to follow her and look after her, so she wandered about—as if in a daze—before she decided to turn around and go back to where she had left the king and queen. She was taken aback for just a second when she entered the room and found her brother standing talking to them. Her first impulse was to run to him and hug him and weep with grief and joy, but she stopped herself, knowing such an action would give her away. He turned and saw her and then ran to her and wept when he realized what had happened to her. She sang to him, as she did to the others. She talked nonsense about flowers, telling him that she would give him some violets, "But they all withered away the day my father died." Then she sang a song about her father's death and left them once again.

Now there was just one last thing she had to do.

• • •

She closed her eyes and stepped into the water. It hurt so much, but she did it again with her other foot. Slowly she walked forward, the cold water rising higher and higher with each step, until it surrounded her and she could no longer breathe. A calmness fell over her and she waited. It didn't take long and when it was over, all her questions had been answered.

• • •

She opened her eyes. She was standing by the pond. The sun had risen. She looked down and saw her body floating lifelessly in the water.

This is how it feels to be dead, she thought to herself. *It feels like...nothing. Neither bad nor good, simply what it is.*

It is a feeling that does not last, she heard another voice speak inside her mind. *Soon you will know grief and despair and regret the choices you made in your sad short life.*

She turned away from the pond and saw the shimmering emerald spirit of her mother. The dream she had forgotten flooded back into her memory and she remembered what had happened that night, which now seemed to have occurred so long ago.

I warned you of what would happen, but you did not listen, her mother's spirit chastised her. *The powers that govern us gave you a gift and you squandered it because of your childish devotion to a man you knew to be a fool! Look in the water! Look in it and see what would have happened if you had listened to my warning and disobeyed your father as I had asked.*

Meekly she turned back towards the pond and look down into it. The water began to bubble and froth as if possessed by some magic force, and when it finally settled she saw herself with the prince in the lobby of the castle. She watched as the prince handed her a gift and she accepted it. She unwrapped it and was delighted to find a collection of poetry the prince had once read from to her. She thanked him and rewarded his generosity with a kiss to the cheek. He blushed and took the book from her and opened it to show her his favorite poem and the two of them read it aloud together.

That was the moment your love became something more than a mutual attraction, her mother's spirit told her.

The image in the water changed and was replaced by various quiet moments of the two of them together.

You brought him peace, explained her mother's spirit as the images came and went. *As much as he mourned the death of his father and the remarriage of his mother, he did not act out. Instead, he logically deduced what had happened to his father with a calm and rational reasoning. He found evidence that proved his uncle murdered his father and showed it to the court. Found out, the king wept in his throne, as weakly as if he were a child. He was deposed and executed, and the prince was made the king. He proved to be a great ruler and easily defeated those from other lands who would try to conquer his people.*

The image in the water became that of a huge and ornate wedding celebration.

He asked you to be his queen and you agreed. You bore him four children, three boys and a girl. Your father lived until his 70th year and you lived to your 86th. In that time he had easily forgiven you for disobeying him all those years ago. He admitted to you that he had wrongly judged the nature of the prince's affections and that it was wrong for him to interfere.

She looked down at the final image of the water, which was of her and the prince and their children laughing and playing together in the lobby of the castle.

This is what you sacrificed by ignoring my warning! This is what you made certain never happened. Look at it and remember! This is what you could have had!

With that the water began to bubble and froth once more and the image disappeared.

She fell to her knees and began to weep.

But my father's ghost, she started to protest.

That was not your father's spirit, the ghost of her mother insisted. *He spoke and the dead cannot speak. It is only through our thoughts that we can communicate.*

Then what was he? she asked as she trembled and wept.

A demon, like that which visited the prince, answered her mother's spirit. *Filled with your love, the prince would have been able to see that the plan given to him by the demon in his father's shape would only lead to misery for all. He would have found his own way to usurp his uncle, but without it he did exactly as it pleased. And so did you.*

I did not know! she cried. *How could I have known!*

If you had listened to your heart! It told you to ignore your father, but you refused to listen, her mother's spirit answered coldly.

Her sobs grew so powerful, she could no longer speak. Her mother's spirit floated towards her and placed a warm arm around her shoulder.

I'm afraid that there is nothing that can be done, the mother whispered to her child. *The powers that govern us can be as cruel as they can be kind, and they do not show any mercy to those that reject their help. You are to be punished for the choices that you made and the punishment is severe.*

What is it? she asked through her tears.

You are going to stay here and watch as what you have wrought comes to pass. You will watch as everyone you love dies and the kingdom you knew forever ceases to be.

Is that all?

It is enough.

• • •

Her body was found, and it was the queen who told her brother that she was dead. They buried her and she watched. The prince was there in the cemetery, having escaped from the boat on which he had been sent away. Her brother wept for her, until he saw the prince and the only emotion he could convey was the most righteous kind of anger.

She watched as her brother and the king conspired to kill the prince. Her brother was going to find justice by fighting with the prince with crossed swords, but he and the king would not let the outcome be settled by either skill or chance. They poisoned her brother's sword. One scratch from it would be enough to prove fatal.

Even this was not enough. The king poisoned his wine and offered it to the prince before the duel began. The prince refused it, and he battled with her brother in front of the eyes of the entire court. Even breathless he refused his uncle's wine again, but his mother did not. The queen took the cup and drank from it.

She watched as the king watched his wife drink from what he knew was a poisoned cup. He did not shout or swat it out of her hands, knowing that to do so would give away his evil plan. Instead he said nothing, and she wondered how he would pay for this horrible crime when he faced the afterlife.

The fight continued, and her brother landed a blow. The prince was wounded, but it was only a scratch, so he continued, not knowing he now had only minutes to live. During the fight, the prince managed to steal her brother's sword and used it against him. He too landed a blow. It was more serious, but that did not matter.

The queen became sick. It was obvious to all what was happening to her. Lying wounded on the floor, her brother confessed what he and the king had done. The queen died, and an enraged prince forced the wicked king to drink from his own poisoned cup. The king died and so did her brother. The prince was the last to go. It didn't take long.

She watched as an army descended upon the castle. A man she had never seen before entered the court, followed by his men. The man bade them carry the prince away and they did.

• • •

Her mother had been wrong. This punishment had not been enough. As the years passed and she watched the world she had made possible happen before her, she did not feel the despair she knew she should have. She wanted to. Regret consumed her, but she knew that regret consumed almost everyone and that it was an emotion so common only a fool would be tortured by it. She felt sad about what she might have had, but not too sad, because she had never known the happiness that would have come with it. It was a gentle melancholy, little different than that which most people feel when their thoughts turn blue. If this was her punishment, then—she decided—it was punishment meted out to both the living and the dead. True, she would have to endure it longer than a living person. Forever sounded like a long time, but after a while it no longer seemed as forbidding.

Ten centuries passed, and she could no longer see the effect her decision had on her kingdom because her kingdom was now nothing like she had ever known. As she watched it, it occurred to her that it was a good kingdom and that she could not imagine how it could have been any better. It was then she realized that maybe she had been right to ignore her mother's warnings. The consequences were dire for herself and her family, but they were now only history and it seemed selfish to her to mourn what had happened to them. Her regret grew smaller and smaller each day. Her melancholy turned to good cheer and her punishment became her reward.

And it was because of this that whenever she thought about how cold the water had been, a smile would warm her face.

Only Pretend

SERENA ROLLED HER EYES AS THE young actress she was dressing grimaced with pain.

"Does it 'ave to be so bloody tight?" whined Bonnie, her thick northern accent at odds with her posh pale blonde features.

"Yes, it does," Serena answered unsympathetically as she pulled the laces of the woman's corset tighter and tighter.

"But I can't 'ardly breathe!"

"Of course you can't," Serena agreed, "but you're going to look lovely."

"It don't matter 'ow I look if I'm bleedin' deceased," argued Bonnie.

"Don't worry," Serena sighed, "I've dressed hundreds of you girls in costumes like this and only one of you has ever died. And we're pretty sure she was a drug addict."

The actress' eyes widened even further at this, suggesting to Serena that she had just touched a nerve.

"I'm joking," she admitted to the woman, even though what she said had been at least partially true.

"That's not bloody funny," Bonnie swore angrily.

"Sorry," Serena muttered apologetically.

"I can 'ave you off for that. I've got the producer's ear, if you understand my meaning."

"Which one?"

"Which ear?"

"Which producer?" Serena sighed.

"Sir 'ume's son. Timothy."

Serena laughed.

"What's so bleedin' funny?" asked the actress.

"He does get around, that Timothy. I doubt there's been a single actress in one of his pictures who hasn't had his ear."

"What do you mean?"

Serena stifled a grin and continued lacing up the corset.

"I'm guessing that this is your first film, right?" she asked.

"That's right."

"You were a model before this."

"For just over a year now, yeah."

"And just a few weeks ago your agent got a call from the son of the president of Anvil Pictures, requesting that you take a screen test for the starring role in their latest production."

"That's what 'appened exactly," the young woman admitted.

"Sure is easier than going up to a girl at a club and chatting her up, isn't it?" Serena smirked.

"'E does this all the time does 'e?"

"Only every time we make a picture."

Bonnie frowned.

"'E told me I was special," she pouted.

Serena gritted her teeth with effort as she pulled on the corset's laces and tied them together.

"Sure, you're special," she said to Bonnie, "you're all special. Until the next picture, that is."

With that said she grabbed Bonnie's dress from a hanger and slid it over the actress' head.

"Now don't you look lovely?" she asked the deflated beauty.

Bonnie looked up and took a look at herself in the room's mirror.

"I don't look 'alf bad," she admitted.

"Told you the pain was worth it. Look at that cleavage! Couldn't get that any other way."

"It is eye-catching, isn't it?"

"The camera's going to love it. Now get out of here and get your hair and makeup done. Freddie's probably having a fit right now."

Bonnie turned and—her movements greatly restricted by her costume—slowly walked out of the room. Serena wasn't alone for 10 seconds before someone else walked in needing a costume. He was a tall, thin man with pale skin and dark hair that fell to his shoulders. The first thing Serena ever noticed about a person was how they were dressed, and she was quite impressed by what he was wearing. His clothes were stylish without being fashionable, and they were exquisitely tailored to match his slender frame.

"You're a looker, aren't you?" she smiled at him.

He smiled at this, but stayed silent.

"What can I help you with?" she asked him.

He spoke very slowly and carefully and made no attempt to hide a thick eastern European accent.

"They told me to see you about a costume," he explained.

"I knew that," Serena laughed. "That's what I do! I meant, what sort of costume do you need? What part are you playing?"

"I am to be a villager."

"You? That seems a waste. You're a damn sight handsomer than that chubby fellow they got playing the lead. Fattest Dracula I've ever seen. Did you audition for that part?"

"No. I am not an actor," the man admitted.

"Aren't you? You could be."

"I haven't the talent for it," he explained.

Serena snorted with laughter.

"That's never stopped a person from getting a part in an Anvil picture!" she said to him.

"I have never seen one of these films," the man admitted.

"Consider yourself lucky!" Serena laughed. "An Anvil picture is good for just two things, blood and breasts. Both of which are very cheap to produce."

"I take it you have worked with this company for a while?"

"Since the beginning," said Serena, "back when old Sir Hume actually tried to make quality pictures. Poor sod."

She turned and searched through her collection of villager costumes.

"Don't have much left here. I dressed all the other villagers two hours ago. How tall are you?" she asked him.

"I am six feet and four inches," he answered.

Serena whistled with disbelief.

"The only folks we get around here that tall are the ones playing the monsters." She pulled a costume from the rack and handed it to him. "That's going to be extra tight on you, but it's the biggest I got."

"Is there somewhere where I can change into it?"

"Modest, are we? Don't worry, I've seen it all."

Hesitantly the handsome young man took off his tailored clothes and replaced them with the tattered villager costume. He carefully placed his own outfit on the hanger and gave it to Serena who hung it up.

"It is very tight," he agreed.

"But it looks fine," she told him. "You're going to be the handsomest villager in the mob. I'm sure you'll get a torch and everything."

"I am looking forward to it. It should be most interesting."
Serena laughed.

"You really never have been on a film set before, have
you?" she said before she shooed him out of the room. "You
better get back to the set before Freddie starts screaming.
I hear the picture's already behind schedule thanks to
Timothy's latest 'discovery.' "

With the young man gone, Serena was alone for the first
time in hours. She whipped out a cigarette and took a long drag
on it. Then she walked over to the nightdress she was working
on. It was the one Bonnie would wear in the scene where she
gets seduced and bitten by the count. Serena lifted it up and
held it over her body and looked into the mirror. It suited her.

Working every day with the type of willowy young
woman who was a constant fixture in the ads that appeared
all over the media these days, it was sometimes easy for
Serena to forget that she was a very attractive woman. She
had just turned 34 a month earlier, but—despite her passion
for cigarettes—she could easily claim to be 10 years younger.
Her hair was long and red, but few people knew that, because
she habitually kept it tied up in a tight bun, which she fre-
quently covered with some sort of hat. She liked hats,
because they were old-fashioned and reminded her of a time
when elegance was the rule rather than the exception.
Because her job required her eyes to always be at their best, a
pair of black horn rim glasses was a constant fixture on her
face, which went a long way towards explaining why so few
of her coworkers noticed just how attractive she was. For
though she never looked like how she would dress a character
described as a "spinster librarian," her personal fashion choices
did go a long way towards disguising her obvious appeal.

Serena had no idea why she insisted on hiding her beauty in this manner, though she sometimes wondered if it was because in her heart she knew she could never compete with the actresses she worked with day after day. Her hats and glasses and loose comfortable clothes were her way of surrendering to a battle she was certain she could not win.

With a final exhalation of smoke, she stubbed out her cigarette in an ashtray and walked out of the room to go to the set, on the off chance her services would be needed.

When she got there, she found the villager extras chatting amiably in a small mob inside the dank basement set. She noted with a smile that the tall handsome newcomer had been given a torch, just like she had said he would.

Freddie, the director, was shouting at Davey, his cameraman, for being too slow while Davey shouted back at Freddie for being too impatient. Timothy, the producer and Sir Hume's son, was busy trying to calm down his noticeably angry lead actress, who apparently didn't appreciate being just another notch in the spool of his reel. Cyril, the overweight Shakespearean actor who was assigned the near-impossible task of transforming himself into the image of a suave, sophisticated vampire lord, was at the tea tray stuffing himself with a handful of small finger sandwiches.

"It's going to be another classic from Anvil," Serena sighed as Davey vented his frustration with Freddie by shouting at his gaffers. She looked over and saw that Cyril had managed to cover his costume with a mass of crumbs and ran over to him to clean him up before Freddie saw him and had a fit.

"Thanks luv," said Cyril. "Never did quite get into the habit of being a tidy eater."

"You might want to go see Moira," Serena suggested, referring to Cyril's makeup woman, "you've got some crumbs on your foundation."

He nodded and ran off to get his makeup retouched. At that exact moment Freddie and Davey decided they were ready to film and found themselves without a Dracula.

"Where the bloody hell is he?" swore Freddie.

"Probably heard an ice-cream trolley tinkling outside," answered Davey.

"That's it!" Freddie erupted, before he ran over to Timothy. "You knew I didn't want to cast that fat git! Now he's holding up production! How can you expect me to get this picture in on time and on budget if you insist on hiring incompetents in both of the leads!" With this he pointed his finger over at Bonnie, not caring if his sentiment might hurt her feelings.

"Calm down Freddie," said Timothy, but it was too late. Once Freddie got started on a rant there was no stopping him.

"I don't care if he did train at bloody R.A.D.A.! I don't care if her picture has sold a million bottles of mouthwash! I need people who can do what I say when I say it without making complete asses out of themselves!"

Bonnie burst into tears and ran off the set, just as Cyril returned from the makeup room.

"What's going on?" he asked as his co-star ran past him.

"You can't tell me that that's what Dracula looks like!" Freddie shouted, pointing at him. He then took a quick look around the set and noticed the tall extra holding the torch. "That's what Dracula looks like!"

"I don't have to put up with that!" harrumphed Cyril.

"Then don't!" shouted Freddie.

"Timothy," Cyril turned towards the young producer, "I refuse to work with this raging buffoon. Either he goes or I do!"

Timothy sighed and wearily ran his fingers through his long blond hair. His father had considered casting the classically trained actor to be a personal coup, but Freddie was by far their best director and they simply couldn't afford to get rid of him.

"Fine," he sighed. "You're absolved of the obligations of your contract, Cyril. You have my permission to quit without fear of us taking any legal action against you."

Cyril deflated before everyone's eyes as he realized his bluff had just been called. He paused and tried to think of something to say, but—not wanting to look weak or desperate—he instead just turned angrily away and stormed off the set.

"Thanks Freddie," Timothy gritted his teeth, "now what are we going to do? You've just managed to get rid of our two leads."

Freddie smiled. Problems like this were why he loved being a director.

"Don't worry about it, laddo," he said to Timothy. "It'll just take two days for us to make up for the scenes we'll have to re-shoot."

"But what about the time we'll lose recasting the bloody parts?" Timothy shouted at him.

Freddie turned towards the extras and shouted out to one of them.

"Oy! You with the torch!"

The handsome young man in the tight-fitting costume pointed to himself, to make sure it was he the director was referring to.

"Yes, you," Freddie nodded, "tell me you want to suck my blood."

Confused, the man looked around to make sure this wasn't some kind of joke before he repeated what Freddie had just asked him to.

"I want to suck your blood," he said, his accent working wonders with the words.

"He's perfect," Freddie turned back to Timothy.

"But who is he?" asked Timothy.

"What does it matter?" asked Freddie. "He looks great and he has the accent and he'll do what I say without asking a load of foolish questions."

"But I can't put that on a poster, can I?" argued Timothy.

Freddie rolled his eyes at the young producer.

"No one comes to see these pictures because they care about who is playing Dracula. They just want to see some pretty girls getting bit in the neck while wearing translucent nightgowns with plunging necklines."

"Yes, I know that," Timothy seethed, "but unless I can convince Bonnie to come back we won't have a pretty girl in the picture who can wear a translucent nightgown, plunging neckline or not!"

"Come on," Freddie laughed, "there's got to be hundreds of young girls out there just panting for a leading role in a movie."

For the next few minutes, the two men argued back and forth like this until finally they agreed that Freddie would continue shooting the crowd scenes, while Timothy attempted to find a replacement for Bonnie. Serena was amused by the producer's predicament. While it was true that many actresses would die for a leading role in a movie, no matter how cheap it was, she knew that over the years Timothy had somehow alienated almost all of the women who were endowed with the necessary physical requirements of the role. There was a reason he often resorted to hiring models who had never acted before, and that was because they were the only ones willing to work for him—and once they did, they invariably vowed to never do it again.

"Serena!" Freddie shouted over to her when he and Timothy were finished arguing. She started walked over to him, as he gestured to his new leading man to come meet them. "I'm going to need a proper Dracula costume for"—he turned towards the young man—"what's your name?" he asked him.

"Milos," the man answered.

"Right. I'm going to need a proper costume for Milos here. He's a tall customer, so how soon can you swing it?"

Serena thought about it.

"Well, he's about the same height as Christopher," she said, referring to an actor who had previously played the part in several movies, "and I've got a bunch of his old costumes in a box somewhere. They should fit Milos with just a few alterations. I can do it in about a hour or an hour and a half."

"Take two," said Freddie. "It'll take us at least that to finish the crowd scenes. Maybe even three at the rate Davey is moving today."

"Get stuffed!" shouted Davey, who had been listening from afar.

While the two men began to argue playfully with each other, Serena whisked Milos away, so she could get him into costume.

"See," she smiled at him as they walked, "I told you that you could be a lead in one of these pictures."

"These men," Milos mused, "they seem very emotional."

"Well," she admitted, "as hard as it may be to believe, we here at Anvil are artists of a sort. We can get quite passionate when we want to."

"Passion," said Milos. "It is a good thing."

"I think so," Serena agreed as she opened the door to her work area and let him in.

A few minutes passed quietly as Serena went through some boxes to find the costumes she had told Freddie about. Milos stood silently in the middle of the room and watched her as she searched.

"Your hair," he spoke to her, breaking the silence, "it is red."

"That's right," she nodded.

"I once knew a woman with hair the same color as yours."

"Really? Was she a friend?"

He shook his head.

"A lover," he answered.

Serena blushed.

"Why do you hide it away like that?" he asked her.

"I don't know," she shrugged. "I just like hats, I guess."

"It is a shame to hide something that beautiful away from the world. It is selfish."

Serena laughed at this.

"Do you talk to all of the girls like that?" she asked him.

"I only speak the truth," he insisted.

"Here they are!" she exclaimed a bit too loudly as she finally came across the costumes she had been looking for. Her enthusiasm had a lot less to do with being genuinely thrilled about finding the clothes, than it did with the way it allowed her to change the subject. As flattering as Milos' words were, she simply wasn't used to being spoken to in that way.

"Here, try this one on," she ordered as she handed him a dark pile of clothes.

Milos nodded and removed his villager costume. Serena hadn't paid attention the last time he had undressed in front of her, but this time she couldn't help herself. After a few seconds she became terrified that she was staring at him and quickly averted her gaze and pretended to be occupied by another matter while he put on the Dracula costume.

"How does it look?" he asked when he was done.

She turned back to look at him and tried not to gasp when she saw him. There in the regal (if a bit wrinkled) dark suit and black cape stood not a man dressed like Dracula, but a man who was Dracula.

"It fits you perfectly," she marveled. "Like it was made for you."

"So it does not need to be altered?"

"Not at all," she answered him. "I can't believe it. You and Christopher were pretty much the same height, but I didn't think you too were that close physically."

"It is very comfortable," he admitted. "Especially the cape."

"You look wonderful. Now take it all off."

"Pardon me?" he asked, taken aback.

"I have to wash and press it," she explained. "It'll only take 45 minutes."

"I see," he said.

He removed the costume and handed it to her. She avoided looking at him and handed him a dressing gown to wear in the meantime.

"Head over to makeup," she told him. "By the time they're done with you, your clothes should be ready."

He nodded silently and disappeared out the door.

Serena practically ran to where she kept her cigarettes and lit one as quickly as she could. She nearly inhaled the whole thing in one go, and stubbed it out just a few seconds later. She went to work and put his costume into her washing machine. As it spun and whirred, she looked at herself in the room's mirror and took off her hat. On an impulse she lifted out her hairpins and the bun her hair was in fell apart. She shook her head and used her hands to untangle it and let it fall past her shoulders.

She stared at herself for a very long time.

"It really is beautiful," she whispered to herself, before she became aware of how foolish she was acting and quickly tied her hair back up and threw her hat back onto her head. The clothes were done, so she put them into the dryer and then— once they were ready—she ironed them and hung them on a hanger. By the time she was done, her face betrayed no evidence of the moment she had experienced just a few minutes earlier.

Milos came back from makeup, not looking that much different than he had before he left, and put his costume back on. With the suit and cape cleaned and ironed, the effect it had on him was even more powerful than it had been before.

"Is there anything else?" he asked, as he buttoned up the last button.

"Just these," she said as she handed him an amulet to wear around his neck and a small jewel box.

He slipped the amulet over his head and opened the case.

"What are these?" he wondered.

"Those are your fangs," she explained. "Technically the makeup people are supposed to handle them, but there's only half a brain to be shared among that lot and they keep losing them."

Milos still looked confused.

"You just slip them over your front canines," she went on.

For a second his face remained bewildered until finally the look was replaced by a small, enigmatic smile. It was the type of smile you would most likely see on a person who has been reminded of their lost innocence by coming across a toy they had once played with as a child.

"These are not real," he said, stating the obvious.

"That's right," she nodded, wondering if maybe his strange reaction was the result of a cultural difference she did not understand.

He closed the box and slipped it into his jacket's right-hand pocket.

"Am I ready?" he asked her.

"As you'll ever be," she answered him. "You can go back to the set now, but make sure you're super quiet in case they are filming. Freddie and Davey will kill you if you mess up one of their shots.

"That will be no problem," he told her. "I am very good at keeping quiet. It is a skill I have developed over the passing years."

She laughed.

"The way you say that it sounds like you've been around forever," she teased him, "and you've got to be at least five years younger than I am."

Milos just smiled at this before he silently turned away and returned to the set.

Serena was about to follow him when Timothy walked into the wardrobe room and stopped her. For some reason he seemed excited, like he had just had an epiphany.

"Why didn't you tell me?" he asked her. "All these years and we were all completely blind to it! It's like somewhere in the prop department there's a priceless King Louis armchair and we never noticed it because someone threw a slipcover over it."

"What are you talking about?" she asked him.

"A half hour ago," he answered, "I slipped my head into here to ask you a question and there you were."

"And that surprised you?"

"No," his face broke into a huge grin, "it was what you were doing. You were looking at yourself in the mirror."

Serena's face turned scarlet as she realized she had been caught in her moment of foolish vanity.

"Your hair was down," he continued. "I've never seen you with your hair down."

"I was just being silly," she tried to explain herself. "Milos made a comment and—"

"You were stunning!" Timothy interrupted her. "Why didn't you tell us you looked like that? Why did you hide it from us for so long?"

Serena's embarrassment turned to anger.

"I don't appreciate being made fun of," she chastened him.

"I'm serious!" he insisted. "You're gorgeous, Serena! You're easily as beautiful as any actress who has ever appeared in any one of our movies."

She stared backed at him in stunned amazement.

"Why are you telling me this?" she asked him.

"Because after I saw you it became clear to me that you're the solution to our problem!"

"Are you joking? I swear I will hurt you very badly if you are joking!"

"Why won't you believe me?" he asked her.

"Because if you're about to ask me what I think you're about to ask me, it's absurd. Things like this only happen in the schlock this company produces. They don't happen in real life."

Timothy laughed at this.

"Yeah," he admitted, "but have you ever thought that the reason we produce this schlock is because we want to believe in it? I mean, if we can't make it happen, who can?"

"But I've never acted before," she argued.

"When has that ever stopped us?" he argued back.

"Who will take care of the wardrobe department?"

"Surely, you must know someone who can take it over from you."

"My sister, Claire, I suppose."

"There you go. Call Claire and tell her to get over here right away."

"But Timothy, this is insane. You can't do this!"

"Why not? Movie stars used to be discovered like this all the time! Lana Turner was discovered sitting at a Hollywood soda fountain."

"That's just a myth," she told him, "something the studio publicists told the public because it was a good story."

"So what? I still believe it, even if it isn't true."

"But I don't know if I can do it."

"Listen," he spoke to her calmly, "we can take this one step at time. Call your sister and when she gets here, we'll get you into costume and makeup. Then we'll shoot a screen test. If it's obvious that you're awful, then we'll forget all about it."

"Promise?"

"You have my word. Now get your sister over here."

Serena called Claire, who—despite the unexpectedness of the request—agreed to come to the studio right away. Serena grew more and more anxious as the minutes passed, certain that she was going to make a horrible fool of herself in front of the people she had been working with since she was 16.

"What's this all about?" asked Claire when she got there.

"Timothy wants me in the movie," explained Serena.

"Oh, that's nice of him to give you a cameo after all these years. I'll have to tell everyone to look out for you."

"They won't have to look hard."

"What do you mean?"

"He doesn't want me for a cameo, he wants me for the lead."

"Is he insane?" asked Claire.

"Well, obviously. I think the pressure from his dad has finally driven him around the bend."

"And you're seriously going to do it?"

"Of course not, but the only way I could get him to go was to agree to a screen test. Once they see how awful I am, he'll come to his senses. I'm certain of it."

A few minutes later Serena found herself at the opposite end of a situation she had been in a thousand times before.

"Does it have to be so bloody tight?" she swore as Claire laced up her corset.

"Of course it does," her sister answered.

"No wonder they all hated me so much," she realized as the undergarment dug into her skin and squeezed all of the air out of her lungs. "This is bloody torture."

"Yes," her sister said, nodding, "but you'll have amazing cleavage."

Serena grunted wordlessly at this, now certain that nothing she could imagine was worth this sort of discomfort. That is until she caught a look of herself in the mirror and was mightily impressed.

"Wow!" she gasped aloud.

"Told you," smiled Claire as she tied up the laces. She then grabbed the dress and slipped it over Serena's head.

Timothy popped his head in to see how they were doing.

"You look great!" he told her. "Now we just have to get you through hair and makeup and we can unveil you to Freddie. I can't wait to see his face when he sees you."

"Haven't you told him?"

"All he knows is that I found somebody. I never told him who and he was too busy getting shots of our new Dracula to ask."

Moira and Helen from the makeup and hair departments were shocked when Serena walked in on them in full costume. Timothy was right behind her and ordered them to give her the full glamour treatment. Their shock doubled as they went to work and discovered just how glamorous their coworker really was.

"I wouldn't believe it if it weren't for my own eyes," marveled Moira from makeup as she painted Serena's lips a dark and inviting red.

"It's as if you're a whole new person," agreed Helen, who had simply combed out Serena's long red hair before judging it perfect and in need of no other alteration.

When they were finished, Serena stood up and looked at herself in a full-length mirror. There was no denying it; she looked exactly like the leading lady of an Anvil horror picture.

Timothy was giddy as he led her onto the set. Freddie and his crew were filming a shot of one of the villagers demanding Dracula's blood, but the shot was ruined when the villager caught a glimpse of the redheaded beauty who had just appeared off-camera and suddenly couldn't remember his line. He tried several times to get the words out, but they just wouldn't come.

"Cut!" shouted Freddie, who was obviously irritated by the man's sudden loss of composure. He turned to see what had caused it and nearly fell over when he did.

"Timothy," he spoke, "where on Earth did you find this young goddess?"

Serena blushed.

"Stop it, Freddie," she ordered gently, "I'm far too nervous to take your teasing."

The silence that followed her speaking aloud was all consuming. Everyone stopped when they realized who the redhead really was.

"Serena? Is that you?" The stunned awe in Freddie's voice was genuine. He had had no idea that Timothy's discovery had been the woman he had worked with for years.

"Of course it is," she said. "Who else would it be?"

"I thought it might have been Raquel bloody Welch, but she became too famous for the likes of us years ago," he answered her. "How did this happen?" he asked a beaming Timothy.

"Call it a wondrous result of the magic of pure serendipity," the young producer grinned.

"I only agreed to a screen test," Serena explained to Freddie. "If I'm dreadful I'm not doing it."

Freddie smiled and nodded. He turned and shouted at Davey.

"Get the camera ready! I want full-on glamour lighting. We're going to see whether or not our wardrobe mistress is a star!"

A half hour passed as Davey and his crew moved the camera and set up the lights in the studio's large drawing room set. Freddie gave Serena a few pages from the script and told her to memorize them as best she could. Blessed with a nearly photographic memory, Serena looked over her lines twice and knew them cold. She looked over and saw Milos standing quietly in a dark corner, observing the gleeful mayhem her appearance was causing on the set. Freddie called them both over and asked them to stand in front of the camera while Davey adjusted his lights. They stood there for another 20 minutes. Milos looked uncomfortable under the hot lamps.

"Are you okay?" Serena asked him.

"I am fine," he answered. "I just prefer to be in the dark. It has become my habit."

"I've been dying to ask you about your accent," she admitted. "Where are you from?"

"I was born in Romania," he told her, "but I haven't lived there for a very long time."

"Oh, so you live here in England?"

He shook his head.

"I am just visiting," he said. "I like to travel. I find it hard to stay in one place for very long. How about you?"

"I've never been off the island," she admitted.

"There is no shame in that," he told her. "If you have a home, there is nothing wrong in staying there."

"Yeah, but the truth is I've never really felt like I was at home here. This is just where I've always been. It's not like I feel particularly attached to it."

"Then what is keeping you here?"

"I don't know. Fear, I guess."

"Fear of what?"

She thought about this and smiled.

"Monsters, I suppose," she answered him.

He smiled back.

"There are just as many monsters here as there are anywhere else," he told her. "I know that for a certainty."

Serena was about to respond to this when she was interrupted by a shout from Freddie.

"Quiet you two," he ordered them. "We're ready."

They both turned quiet and listened as Freddie gave them a few simple directions.

"Aren't we going to rehearse?" she asked him when he told them to begin.

"What do you think this is?" he asked her.

"But you're rolling."

"Just because we call it a rehearsal doesn't mean we can't use it if it's any good," Freddie explained.

"Use it? But we agreed this is a screen test."

"Sure it is," Freddie nodded. "And if you're indescribably awful, than we'll burn the negative and never speak of it again. But if you're good, then that means we have one less scene to put on the schedule. Now, are you two ready?"

They both nodded.

"Okay then," he nodded before he sat down in his chair beside the camera. "Action!" he shouted.

It took Serena a second before she realized this was her cue to begin. In the scene they were both facing the camera, as if they were looking at a portrait on a wall. She turned to Milos and said her first line.

"That was my father. He died when I was just a small child."

"So young?" asked Milos, as he said his first line.

"Yes. He was murdered. They found his body in a back alley in Whitechapel. Someone had cut his throat."

"Whitechapel? Isn't that where that madman murdered all those woman?"

"Yes. For a time they suspected that he might have been the one who did it."

"Really? Why?"

"Because the murders stopped immediately after he was discovered in the alley."

"What a strange coincidence."

"I hope so. Some nights I lie awake and wonder if maybe if he really was the Ripper. It tortures me that I'll never really know for sure."

Milos followed the script's direction and smiled with a charming but wicked grin.

"My dear, I can say with 100% certainty that he was not the Ripper."

"I wish I could believe you."

"Trust me, I know," Milos spoke the scene's last line enigmatically.

"Cut!" shouted Freddie.

"There I told you," sighed Serena. "I was horrible."

"You were fine," disagreed Freddie. "But this time allow yourself to be a little more charmed by the count's presence. You have to seem that you are attracted to him. Can you do that?"

Serena looked over at her handsome costar.

"Yes," she answered truthfully.

"And Milos, I want more of a sense that you are toying with her. Remember, you're the one who killed her father all those years ago and you did it to frame him for all the murders you yourself committed in Whitechapel."

Back when Serena first started she used to go over each script very carefully to see what costumes would be needed for the production, but as the years went on and the films became cheaper and more formulaic, it got so she could just look at the character sheet and instantly know what she needed. As a result, this was the first time she had heard about this particular plot development.

"Excuse me," she interrupted, "but are you saying that in this film Dracula turns out to have been Jack the Ripper?"

"Yes," Freddie nodded.

"But didn't we already do that in one of our Frankenstein movies?"

"Yes," Freddie sighed, "and we also did it in that awful Jekyll and Hyde movie we shot last year."

"Isn't that a bit repetitive?"

"No, it's very repetitive, but it's a good plot twist and I suspect we'll be using it in one of the Mummy movies next."

In the end Serena and Milos replayed the scene four more times until Freddie was satisfied with it. When they were done, Freddie looked at his watch.

"I suppose that's it for today," he decided.

The crew started to finish up for the day, and Freddie and Timothy walked over to their two new stars.

"Well?" Serena asked them impatiently.

They both smiled.

"We'll know for sure when the dailies get back the day after tomorrow," said Freddie, "but I'm certain we'll all be happy with what we see."

"You were very good, Serena," insisted Timothy.

"Yes," agreed Freddie, "and I suspect that the camera will have been very generous to you. It pains me that I never noticed it before, but you have the kinds of features that truly stand out on film."

Serena couldn't help but feel ambivalent about her director's praise. On the one hand, she was enjoying the feeling of living out a strange and melodramatic dream, while on the other she was terrified about what would happen when she woke up and reality came crashing back in around her.

She looked up at Milos and took comfort in the fact that—even though he was living through the exact same dream—he looked completely at ease. She pretended to listen as Timothy explained to her how much she was going to get paid and other routine details. She held her breath and closed her eyes and when she finally exhaled and opened them again, she found herself standing alone with Milos.

"This is so bizarre," she said to him.

"What is?" he asked her.

"This. All of this. Don't you think it's strange?"

"Why should it be strange?"

"Think about it. One minute we're common everyday people and the next we're the stars of a real honest-to-goodness movie."

Milos frowned.

"Serena," he spoke slowly and deliberately "we are not common everyday people. I know for a fact that I am not. And you…You are very special."

"Thank you for saying that, but—"

"There is no 'but,' " he interrupted her. "I have told you that I have traveled and that is the truth. There is not a city or town on this whole continent that I have not seen with my very eyes and I can count on one hand how many women I have met who share the quality that you possess."

"Which is?"

"I have not the words to describe it, in this language or my own, but it is as apparent and obvious to me as a bonfire burning a foot away from my face. These men are fools that it took them so long to notice the heat your presence exudes, but now that they feel it they cannot deny it."

Serena stayed silent. She was stunned by the passion with which Milos spoke.

"But you cannot totally blame them for their folly," he continued. "You tried so hard to hide your power from everyone. You did not trust it or maybe it frightened you, but there was no way you could keep it hidden. It had to be released eventually and today it has been. Forget who you were yesterday, that woman no longer exists. From this moment you are who you were always meant to be."

Listening to Milos, Serena felt tears coming to her eyes. No one had ever spoken to her like this. She could tell that he was not merely saying what he thought she needed to hear, but instead he genuinely believed that she was unlike anyone he had ever known. Not once in her entire life had she ever considered the possibility that she was special, but now, hearing the sincere intensity in this handsome young man's voice, she could not deny that maybe he was telling her the truth.

Without another word, Milos turned from her and walked away. Serena took a moment to calm herself and went back to the wardrobe room and got out of the ridiculously uncomfortable corset with the help of her sister. As she reveled in the end of her agony, she looked over and saw Milos' clothes still hanging where he had left them.

"Hasn't he come in to drop off his costume?" she asked Claire.

"Who? Dracula? I don't think so. The last I saw him, he was walking down into the basement."

"Why would he do that?"

Claire shrugged.

"Not a clue," she admitted.

Serena wondered if she should investigate, but decided that the strange activities of the day had taken their toll on her and she really needed to go home, eat some dinner and go to sleep, which is exactly what she did.

• • •

After that the days passed by so fast that Serena wondered if someone was fooling around with the clocks around her. These films were made on such short schedules, she had little time to prepare or even think about what she was doing. It was lucky she was able to memorize her lines so quickly or else she would have never been able to keep up. Milos also seemed to be affected by the rapid pace of production, but instead of feeling tired, he seemed more invigorated as the days went by.

A week had gone by and Serena realized that she had been so busy that she had no idea what was happening outside the studio. Thankfully, she was given a break when Freddie spent the ninth day on the schedule filming all the exterior scenes featuring the rampaging mob of peasants. She used the day to stay home and read some newspapers and listen to the radio. She was shocked to learn that over the past few days the city had been plagued by a rash of strange murders. All the victims were known criminals, and the police believed the person responsible was some kind of vigilante. The strangest thing about the incidents was that all the victims had bled to death, but not a drop of blood was found next to their bodies. Serena felt a chill run down her spine as she read this and turned to the entertainment section, wanting to get away from the grim reality of everyday life. She almost jumped when she saw her own picture in the paper. "A Fairy Tale Story" the headline read as the story beneath it described how she had ended up being cast in the movie.

"Timothy will like that," she smiled to herself, knowing that it had been years since an Anvil movie had done anything to get noticed by the journalistic media. She was right, her hunch confirmed when he called her just a few minutes later.

"Did you see your picture in the papers today?" he asked before she even had time to say hello.

"I saw the one in the *Times*. Am I in any others?" she asked him.

"You're in all of them! It's amazing. This is the best publicity we've had in years."

The next day, when Serena returned to the studio, several reporters hung around the set and asked her as many questions as they could come up with. Timothy had invited them over hoping to keep the story alive for as long as he could.

Freddie was annoyed by the intrusion on his set, but he was too busy to do anything about it. Today they were filming the sequence where Serena's character discovers that the handsome nobleman she has fallen in love with is really the infamous Count Dracula.

She was talking to one of the reporters when she saw Milos walk onto the set. He had his fangs on and looked quite dangerous in a very appealing way. For some reason none of the reporters seemed too interested in talking to her costar, even though his story was almost exactly the same as hers. She excused herself from the reporter and walked over to where Milos was standing, which, typically for him, was a dark corner away from everyone else.

"You're looking good," she complimented him.

"Thank you. I feel well."

"Film-making must agree with you."

"I think it does."

"Are you nervous about today's scenes? Are you ready to become a monster?"

Milos thought about this.

"The job of an actor is to think like the character, yes?" he asked her.

"That's what they say."

"Then I think—as far as my character is concerned—he is not the monster. You are."

"I am?"

"Not you specifically. Humanity. I have been thinking about this and it is clear to me that this man kills because he has to. He needs blood to survive. But humanity, it kills for no reason. To him you are the monsters."

"But he's evil. He was Jack the Ripper. He kills people for sport."

"Perhaps the boredom of immortality has driven him mad. He sees himself surrounded by killers and decides he might as well join in the fun."

"I suppose that could be one interpretation," she admitted doubtfully.

"Do you have another?"

"He's the bad guy."

"Yes," Milos smiled, "that is a more simple way to look at it."

"Simple is what these movies are about. They're not meant to be complex."

"And that is why they are only pretend. Reality is incapable of being anything other than complex."

"I don't know about that," she disagreed.

"Trust me," he insisted. "In this world nothing is simple and nothing is easy."

"Oy!" they heard Freddie shout at them. "Time is money you two! We're ready to film!"

The two of them walked out of the dark corner and watched Freddie as he showed them what he wanted them to do during the shot. They rehearsed it with the camera a couple of times and then filmed it four times before Freddie was satisfied. Each shot ended with a close-up of Milos' teeth as he bared them at Serena, evilly intending to sink them into her neck.

At the end of the last take, Freddie and his crew started preparing for the next shot. Milos walked away from Serena and left the set, heading towards the door that led to the basement. As he moved, Serena noticed he had dropped something, and she bent over to pick it up. It was a small jewel box, just like the one she had given him the first time she dressed him in his costume. She opened it up and was confused by what she saw. It wasn't just like the case she had given him, it was the case she had given him, and in it were the same two fake fangs that had intrigued him when he first saw them.

"If he wasn't wearing these," she whispered to herself, "where did the ones he was wearing come from?"

Knowing she had at least 20 minutes before she was needed again, she went over to the makeup room and asked Moira and Helen if they had given Milos some new fangs.

They both said no.

• • •

Over the years Serena had spent a lot of time in the studio basement, because it contained hundreds of boxes and cases filled with old costumes. Sometimes she would spend hours going through those boxes looking for something that could be reused or could provide some inspiration. So she was used to the dark damp space and felt no anxiety whatsoever as she walked down the old wooden stairway.

"Milos?" she called out, but he did not respond.

She reached the basement floor and pulled the string that turned on the uncovered bulb that provided the majority of the large space's light.

"Turn it off!" she heard a familiar voice shout out to her, more with annoyance than with anger.

"Milos, is that you?"

"Yes," he answered her. "Turn off that damn light."

She turned it off and felt a presence move towards her in the darkness.

"Serena," he spoke to her, "what do you want?"

"You dropped this," she handed him the jewel box. "Can you see it?"

"Yes," he answered. "I can see very well in the dark."

"It's still full. It still has the fangs inside it."

"I know."

"Did you get new ones?"

"No."

"Then how—"

"Do you really need me to answer that question?"

"Yes."

"I do not need these pretend teeth. My real ones are good enough."

"Are you—"

"Yes. Does that frighten you?"

"Yes."

"Why?" he asked her.

"Because that makes you the bad guy," she answered him.

"If this were a simple, uncomplicated movie, then I suppose it would. But this is not a movie, and I am not a bad man."

"You kill people?"

"Yes."

"Then how can you say that you are not evil?"

"I already told you. The world is a complex place. Yes, I kill. I kill so that I may live. I did not choose for this to be my fate, but it is and I have to accept it."

"You could kill yourself."

"A long time ago I tried. Many times. Of all the mistakes these movies make, the biggest is the ease with which my kind is vanquished. I have felt a stake go through my heart; I have been beheaded; I have been burned alive by the rays of the sun, and each time I have risen, stronger than I was before."

"You could stop drinking blood."

"Then I get hungry, and hunger has a way of turning me into an animal. I must feed to keep my sanity. The last time I tried to abstain from that which my body craves a whole village died in one night. I had stopped because a woman just like you had asked me to. When I finally regained my mind I found her lifeless body in my arms. She was the last of that night's victims."

"You are a monster!"

"No!" Milos shouted. It was the first time she had seen him lose his temper. "I told you! I kill because I must and I feed from those who are truly monstrous! Last night I fed from a man who had killed four people for the change in their pockets! Before that I killed a man who took runaway girls from the streets and turned them into hollow-eyed sexual slaves! They had a choice and they chose to destroy. I do not have a choice!"

"You're the vigilante the police are looking for?"

"I am the one the police are always looking for. I travel not because I want to, but because I have to. In truth I have stayed here too long. There is only one thing keeping me from going."

"The movie?"

"What do I care about some silly fantasy? I thought it might be amusing to pretend to be what I really am, but it isn't. It just reminds me that I can never escape from this life I have found myself in."

"Then why do you stay?"

"It amazes me that you have to ask that. I am here because of you."

"Me?" she whispered.

"You refuse to believe me when I tell you how special you are, but it is the truth. I have spent centuries on this earth and I can count on one hand all of the women I have met who have been your equal. Of them, only one knew the truth about me and I already told you what happened to her."

Serena started to speak when she was interrupted by a voice from above.

"What are you two doing down there in the dark?" asked the voice.

"Nothing," they both shouted together.

"Well stop it. We need you on set. Freddie is having a fit because you're not there."

Milos walked past Serena and started going up the stairs. She found it difficult to move. Over the past few days she thought her concepts of reality had been stretched as far as they could go, but now they were beyond the breaking point and she was afraid of what would happen when they snapped.

She turned around and walked up the stairs. She heard not a single word of Freddie's tirade as she appeared on the set. She looked at Milos, dressed in his costume and could not tell what she was really seeing. Was he a horrible monster or a poor victim of circumstances beyond his control? During the whole scene she did nothing but try to answer this question. In the end she decided he looked like neither. He simply looked lonely. She realized that everywhere he went he had to hide who he really was. She herself had done this for years, for no other reason than her own petty insecurities.

Now that she was free from her disguise, she understood how hard it must be for him knowing that he could never take his off.

She was still consumed by these thoughts when the day ended and everyone went home for the night. Her sides burned with red welts caused by the corset, and she soothed them by soaking in a warm bath. From where she sat she was able to see her reflection in the mirror. She looked at herself and saw someone just as lonely as the monster in the studio. Her disguise was gone, but she did not feel free. All everyone knew now was what she really looked like, nothing more. She lay back in the tub and let the water soak her hair. She looked up at the ceiling and thought about what it must be like to be immortal, to live forever and travel the world. She thought of all the different things he must have experienced over the centuries, which made her think of all the things he might see in the years to come. She closed her eyes and imagined the fashions he had been able to wear and the ones he would wear in the future. She thought of him and felt all of her fear and all of her pity ebb away. She pulled out the bathtub's plug with her big toe, and the water slowly drained away. The cold air felt sharp against her naked skin. She wondered if this was anything like it felt to be dead. If it was, then she liked it.

• • •

It was the last day of filming, which meant that Serena would not have to suffer the discomfort of the dreaded corset because she would be wearing only a white silk nightdress. It suited her. The crew found it hard not to stare.

She went to the bed that was the centerpiece of the whole scene and lay down on it. She closed her eyes and recalled all of the thoughts that had kept her from sleeping the night before. She was in a dream and chances were it could continue if that was what she wanted, but it wasn't. She didn't want her old life either. All her life she had felt like a stranger in this world and now she knew why. It was because there was a man she hadn't met yet and now that she had, she did not want to let him go.

"Are you sleeping?" she heard someone ask. She opened her eyes and saw Milos standing above her.

"If I am, I don't want to be awake," she smiled.

Freddie came over to them and explained to Milos how he wanted him to bend over and bite Serena in the neck. Serena realized that these were not directions that Milos needed to hear.

She felt her body tingle, like it had in the tub. She closed her eyes again and waited for Freddie to call action.

She felt Milos' hands as they touched her body. They were cold and she liked how they felt on her skin. She felt his body lean in against hers and his mouth close around her neck. If just a few seconds ago she was uncertain, now she knew.

"Do it," she whispered so quietly the crew could not hear.

Milos hesitated, unsure of what he just heard.

"Now," she whispered again. "Do it now."

She felt his teeth sink into her neck. She felt her warm blood leave her body as he drank. The feeling was extraordinary, unlike anything she had ever known. She cried out and tears came to her eyes. She opened them and saw the crew watching them from afar. All they saw were two actors performing a scene they had shot a hundred times before, but she knew that this one was unlike any other. It was the first real thing the studio had ever filmed.

"Cut," ordered Freddie, and Milos obeyed him and stopped feeding from her neck. The cuts on her neck closed as soon as his teeth left them.

"One more time," ordered Freddie, "just for safety."

• • •

Serena felt so hungry. She and Milos walked down the dark alley, holding each other's hands. She could hear things she had never heard before. She could see in the dark like it was the day. The air smelled bitter and metallic, heavy with the odor of blood. She was hungry and wanted to feed from the first person they had come across, but Milos wouldn't let her.

"She has done nothing wrong," he explained. "We can find someone more deserving."

She nodded, and they searched around for someone the world would not miss.

In the distance they heard the sounds of a man's cries. It took them just seconds to get to where they had come from.

Two men were kicking another man. Their heads were shaved, and they wore heavy steel-toed boots. They were white, and the man on the ground was black.

"Think you can come into my neighborhood?" one of them sneered as he kicked the man.

"Bloody foreigners!" shouted the other.

Serena looked at Milos with an eager grin.

"These two will do," he said smiling.

Those two men were the last victims the police found that could be attributed to the vigilante. The investigation didn't continue much longer after that. The official explanation was that the case grew cold, but unofficially those in charge feared that the person—or persons—responsible might be scared away and never come back.

Six years later a very attractive young couple walked into a small movie theater located on New York's Times Square. They seemed out of place amongst the theater's usual crowd of junkies, bums and adventurous film buffs. The movie on the screen was a bad vampire flick that no one had seen since it played for the one week it was in release years ago. Most everyone slept and snored their way through it, but the exotic couple sat there and laughed.

To them it was the funniest thing they had ever seen.

Empathy

THERE WAS A FLOOD WARNING FOR the entire state. The rain would not stop coming. Droplets the size of marbles pounded down ceaselessly and soaked everything they touched within seconds. The two MPs who were carrying Private Anderton wore long military issue ponchos, while the private wore only the pants that had come with his uniform. He had ripped everything else off by the time his screams had brought him to their attention.

He wasn't screaming anymore. His voice had given out and now he just wept quietly as the two large men placed him in one of the base hospital's waiting room chairs.

"Should we cuff him?" one asked the other.

"Look at him," his partner answered. "He can barely stand up, much less make a break for it."

A nurse approached them and asked what was wrong. They pointed to the weeping and bedraggled private, and the nurse needed no more explanation. He wasn't the first and she doubted he would be the last.

"I'll call Dr. Sadler," she told them.

The doctor was awakened by the sound of his phone ringing. His wife, Eugenia, answered it and handed him the receiver. She was far too used to these late night calls to be annoyed by them.

"What is it?" asked the doctor, even though he had a good idea of what the problem was. "Uh-huh," he grunted when the nurse told him. "I'll be right there," he sighed.

"Another one?" asked Eugenia with a yawn.

"Looks like it," he said as he started to get dressed.

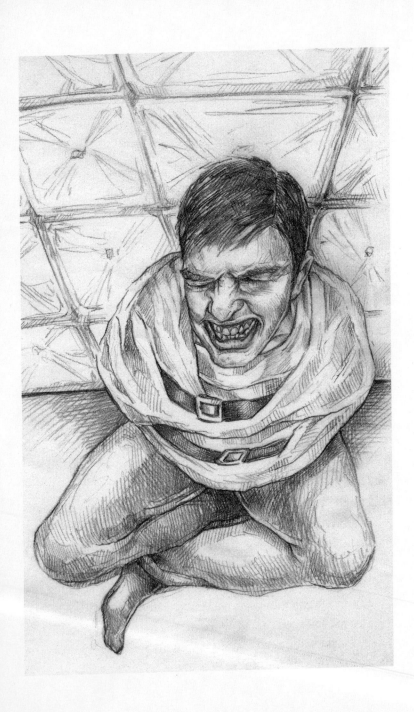

"Isn't there anything that can be done about this?"

Dr. Sadler stopped buttoning up his shirt and looked over to her.

"I don't know," he told her. "I wish I did, but I don't."

Private Anderton was in a straightjacket and locked up in the hospital's rubber room by the time the doctor saw him. Like many of the others, he had started to try to slam the misery out of his mind, and this room was the only safe place for him to do it. Still, even while pounding his skull against the white padding that surrounded him he had managed to draw blood. The doctor ordered that he be given another sedative, and he wiped away the private's blood with his own handkerchief.

As the drug took effect, Anderton stopped moving and sat quietly on the floor with his back against the wall. Tears continued to stream down his face. Without his hands free they had nowhere else to go.

"Andrew..." he sobbed under his breath, his voice still hoarse from the screaming.

"Andrew," Dr. Sadler repeated. He had heard it many times before. "Tell me about Andrew."

"I killed him," Anderton confessed with a sob.

"But it was an accident."

Anderton nodded.

"You were just trying to save him," the doctor continued. "The gun—"

"It exploded in your hands. It wasn't your fault."

Anderton cried even harder than before.

Dr. Sadler crouched down and examined the private's head. Just like the others, there were fingertip-sized burn marks around his temples.

"She was beautiful, wasn't she?" he asked the tortured young man.

Anderton nodded silently as his tears continued to fall.

Dr. Sadler nodded with him. "They all say she was beautiful."

• • •

Floods were coming. The rain would not stop. Melanie's suit was soaked from the rain, but she didn't notice. She was too busy cursing the sky because she was unable to row out to the island until the clouds departed. Her rage kept her warm, but it made it difficult for her to stay quiet. It had been over a year since she had last seen Andrew and it killed her to know that he was only one short boat ride away. The temptation to go out in the rain was strong, but her boat was small and there was no way she could row and bail at the same time. She had to wait. She had never been a patient woman.

• • •

Including Anderton, nine soldiers had been found suffering from the same bizarre dementia. Of that nine, five had managed to commit suicide—despite near constant supervision—and two had died of natural causes—a heart attack and a stroke—both of which had been brought about by the men's madness. Besides the private, the only other surviving victim was a sergeant named Margold. He had wept continuously for three months and looked as though he too was going to try to end his life, but then one day he just stopped. Although he could still walk, and he responded physically to all of the standard stimuli, he took on the attributes of a catatonic. He stopped speaking, and no longer seemed to notice what was happening around him. Dr. Sadler decided to visit him after the sedatives he had given Anderton allowed the private to get some sleep.

The doctor found Margold sitting in his standard position. He sat up on the edge of his cot, with his head forward and his posture ramrod straight. He stared at the wall, his face as blank as its drab white surface.

"Hello, sergeant," greeted Dr. Sadler as he walked into Margold's room, even though he knew the man wouldn't—or couldn't—acknowledge him, "how are we doing today?" He wasn't offended by the silence that followed his polite question.

Unlike Anderton, Margold was an older man in his 40s. He had once been a strong bull of a man, but a year of catatonia had turned his body loose and flabby. The orderly came in to shave him just once a week, and his face was now heavily shadowed by bristly stubble.

Dr. Sadler took out the small flashlight and shone it into the sergeant's eyes. The sergeant blinked, like he always did. The doctor clapped his hands loudly right beside the sergeant's right ear, and the big man flinched like he always did. When a small hammer tapped his knee, his leg reflexively kicked up.

It was because of these reactions that Dr. Sadler believed that the disciplined sergeant wasn't really catatonic, but was protecting himself against the pain and sadness that had killed all the others. Margold's staring out at the wall was not the result of impassivity, but rather a willed effort to not be overcome by his despair.

Dr. Sadler had decided that until he had a better idea of what was causing this psychosis, he would make no attempt to change Margold's condition. He feared that if he interfered, the sergeant would likely end up suffering the same fate as the others.

"Have a good day sergeant," he said as he turned to leave. He wasn't offended that Margold didn't say good-bye.

• • •

As Melanie shivered in the rain, she tried to keep herself warm by enveloping herself with memories of the day she and Andrew first met. Thinking of him always brought a blush to her cheeks, and it kept the cold at bay. She remembered how she felt the first time she saw him at her cousin Annabelle's wedding, where he had served as the groom's best man. At first she had only seen the coarse ruggedness of his features, dominated as they were by his tanned skin and large crooked nose (she would later find out that it hadn't healed correctly after he had broken it during a collegiate boxing match). But then she caught sight of his eyes, which were such a brilliant and unexpected blue that some people were known to gasp when they first saw them.

Melanie was no exception. She gasped, and the sound of her startled exhalation brought her to the attention of the man she was looking at. Andrew looked up at her and saw a woman so striking that she reminded him of the heroines in the fairy tales he had read as a young boy. With her long auburn hair and diamond-etched cheekbones, she easily could have been mistaken for the Fairy Queen. All she needed was a pair of wings, long pointed ears and a dress made of flowers. Having caught his gaze, she smiled at him and he smiled back. It was at that moment they knew—without words—that they were in love.

They were married two months later. Her parents had been charmed by his manners and pleased by his ambition. His family had deep roots in law and politics, and he saw himself running for governor someday. He was also wealthy enough to support their daughter in the manner they felt she deserved.

Melanie herself cared little about his money and would have married him if he had been a poor blacksmith or groomsman. She indicated early on in their relationship that she wasn't impressed by extravagant presents and was instead only interested in the gift of his company. And though his work kept him busy, he made sure he could always find a way to give her exactly what she wanted.

Remembering her disdain for expensive gifts, Andrew decided—on the day of their first anniversary—to take her out for a simple picnic. After they ate, they held each other and waited for the sun to set. As it did, he asked her if there was anything else she wanted.

"No," she answered. "This is all I need."

He kissed her and smiled.

"Then it will be yours every year from now on," he promised her.

"I'll hold you to that," she grinned at him.

"You won't have to," he insisted.

Twilight slowly surrounded them, and they lay there until it faded into the night. They continued to hold each other as they dreamed of future picnics, never considering that this one would be their last.

• • •

"YOU DON'T KNOW THE MEANING OF THE WORD LOVE!" Anderton screamed at Dr. Sadler through his tears. "It's a concept to you. *An abstract idea.* You think that you have felt it, but *you haven't.* If you had you wouldn't need me to explain my pain to you. I KILLED HIM! *Do you understand?* I KILLED MY LOVE! I KILLED ANDREW!"

Dr. Sadler stayed calm. He had heard outbursts like this before.

"How did you kill him?" his voice remained stoically inquisitive.

"You know how!"

"Yes, I know how you killed him, but I want to know how you managed to kill a man who died over sixty years before you were born?" Dr. Sadler had managed to find out this much by combing through the base's records, but beyond a name and date he had no other details.

"What do you mean?"

"Andrew Lanier died in 1864, while he was a prisoner at this base. So, how then were you able to kill him in 1948?"

"I don't understand."

"It's a very simple question. How could you have killed Andrew if he died before you were ever born?"

Anderton looked confused.

"But I can feel it!" he insisted. "I was *there!* I *pulled* the trigger! You don't understand."

"I understand that it seems very real to you. I'm sure you remember every thought and sensation as if it were happening to you right this second, but it isn't. It never has. You never met Andrew Lanier, much less killed him. No matter what your memories tell you, that is never going to change."

"Why are you telling me this?" asked Anderton with a look of hatred in his eyes. "Why are you lying to me? You think I don't know what's going on in here?" he slapped the side of his head to emphasize his point. "I remember! It's in here. I killed him. You don't know," he wept. "You don't know."

• • •

Melanie had tried to convince him to stay.

"What does this war have to do with us?" she asked him, even though she knew his answer.

"Lincoln means to make slaves of us all," Andrew explained. "We fought against the tyranny of the British so we could live our lives the way we want to! If we let the Union states impose their will against us, our revolution will have been for nothing."

"I don't understand," she shook her head. "Especially after all the times I've heard you speak out against slavery."

"This isn't about slavery! It's about freedom! It's about our rights as states to make our own decisions and not be vulnerable to the whims of one man—no matter what his title or office!"

"I don't care how often you explain it to me, it still sounds insane!" she shouted back at him. "You're talking about going to war against *Americans!* I don't care how you justify it, it will always sound like murder to me!"

"This is about our way of life!"

"No! This isn't about how we live. We live for each other. We don't live for them!"

"It is my *duty*."

"Your duty is to stay with me!" she roared at him. "You promised!"

Andrew hung his head.

"I know I did, and nothing tears me up more than knowing I have to break that promise, but there are times when a man has to put his country ahead of himself. This war is greater than the two of us. You may not understand that, but I do."

Melanie stayed quiet. She knew that nothing she could say would change his mind. She ran over to him and hugged him as tightly as she could.

"If you go," she whispered to him, "you must promise me that you will live. No matter what happens to you, no matter how badly you are outnumbered or wounded, you must live. If you don't, I will never forgive you."

"I promise," he whispered back to her. "For as much as I fear what could happen to me in battle, I know enough to fear your wrath that much more."

• • •

After three days the rain still would not stop. Dr. Sadler looked out of his office window and watched as soldiers worked to pile sandbags around the base. He had just received word that the roads were officially closed and that he would have to stay at the base until further notice. He had called Eugenia to let her know and to ease her fears. He reminded her that their house was built at a high enough elevation that it would take a flood as large as that experienced by Noah for it to be endangered, but she didn't sound convinced. They were both grateful that their son, Abbie, was away at a Canadian summer camp.

"It'll all be over soon," he comforted her.

"I know, but it's just so unbearably gothic in this damn house," she complained. "I'm terrified that the power will go out and it'll be like I'm in one of those Boris Karloff movies."

As soon as she mentioned the power going off, Dr. Sadler knew it was only a matter of minutes before her prophecy came true. Eugenia had a gift for knowing when bad things were about to happen. Just half an hour after they hung up on each other, the lights went out. The building's emergency generators kicked in, but their output wasn't that strong. The lights returned, but they flickered and were unusually dim. A call came over the intercom to unplug or turn off any superfluous machinery, but those measures did little to improve the quality of the lights overhead. If Eugenia had thought their house seemed depressingly gothic, he wondered how she would be affected by the hospital's oppressively dark and gloomy atmosphere.

Tired, he took off his shoes and lay down on the small sofa that sat in a corner of his office. Just as he managed to close his eyes, another call came over the loudspeaker. The doctor jumped up when he heard it and ran out of the office, not even bothering to put on his shoes. As fast as he ran, he didn't make it in time. Just a few hours after he had ordered Anderton to be removed from the rubber room and out of his straightjacket, the young private had managed to find a way to end his own life.

• • •

Melanie refused to leave her bed. It had been six months since she had last heard anything from Andrew, and she was certain that he was dead. Her servants tried to care for her as best they could, but she was so despondent, it became more and more difficult for them to get her to eat or even talk to them.

Finally, they were able to rouse her from her stupor when a young Confederate soldier came to the house, claiming to have some news about his commanding officer, Andrew Lanier. They had to carry her out of her bed, she had grown so weak, and the young soldier was shocked by her appearance. He heard stories about a strong and vibrant beauty whose passion could shake the earth, and here he found a gaunt, frail woman who barely had the strength to speak.

After a moment's hesitation, he told her what had happened to her husband and why it had been so long since she had last heard from him.

"He was captured, along with a hundred other men, and is being held prisoner at a Union army base. I was there with him, but through a lucky turn of events I was able to escape. I joined another garrison, and we have set up camp just a few miles from here. When I realized I was so close to your home, I knew I had to come and tell you where your husband was, as he had confided in me his fears about how you were dealing with his absence."

"How was he, the last time you saw him?" her voice was a hoarse rasp.

"As good as could be expected. Conditions for prisoners at the base are poor at best, but the last time I saw him he was strong and healthy enough to serve as a perfect role model for his men."

Melanie thanked the young soldier for his efforts and he left to go back to his garrison's camp. When he was gone, she turned to one of her servants and told her to get the local doctor. When he arrived, it took all of her strength to stand in front of him.

"I have grown weak," she explained, "but now I have to be strong. Tell me what I have to do."

• • •

Sitting alone in his office in the dark hospital, Dr. Sadler carefully reread the notes he had taken over the past two years regarding the men who had all suffered from the same strange delusion. As a man of science, his instincts told him to reject the idea that there might be a supernatural reason for what was happening to these men, but all the evidence he had defied a more conventional explanation. All nine men believed that they were responsible for killing a man who died over 80 years ago. They all claimed to love their supposed victim, a man they never could have met. They all suffered from identical burn marks around their temples, and they all described vague visitations by a beautiful woman dressed in a long dark robe.

Nine men. He had seen examples of group psychosis before, but this one was too specific and its occurrences were too random to fit such a tidy rationalization. There was something— or someone—out there that was responsible for this. Lightning flashed in the rain outside and was closely followed by a crack of thunder. There was just one person who really knew what was going on, and he was too busy staring at a wall to help. Dr. Sadler looked out of his window and watched the pounding rain as it fell angrily to the devastated ground. He had to ask. He knew the possible consequences, but still he had to ask.

• • •

Margold had no window to look out of and had no idea what was happening outside. He thought only about the drab white wall in front of him, and he imagined himself in it, surrounded by an infinity of nothingness. He heard the door to his room open, but he did not turn his head to see who was there. It would either be the doctor, a nurse or an orderly. Whoever it was, it didn't matter; he couldn't let himself be distracted. A face appeared in front of him. It was the doctor. He stared through him and thought only about the wall. The doctor began to speak.

"Who is she?" he asked.

Margold ignored him.

"Why is she doing this? Where were you when she came?"

Margold thought only of the wall, the doctor's questions no match for the silence of its emptiness. He stayed still and silent.

"Answer me!" the doctor shouted at him. "Unless we find a way to stop her, more and more men are going to die—or worse, spend the rest of their lives in their own deliberate oblivion!"

For the briefest of seconds, Margold's mind flashed back to the lady in black. She stood before him, full of remorse, pity and despair. Dressed in a long dark robe, she looked like a creature from a fairy tale. A dark fairy queen. She had smiled at him, but it wasn't a happy smile. It was a sympathetic smile, softened by regret. Her red lips indicated that there would be no pleasure in the suffering she was about to inflict. Even at that moment, when she had brought him so much pain, she had looked more beautiful than anything he had ever seen. She had spoken to him, but he could not remember what she had said. He remembered only the memories she had burned into his mind.

As brief as this flash was, the doctor still saw it in Margold's eyes.

"What did she do?"

Margold tried to stay inside the wall, but his brief moment of reflection allowed his other memories to invade his mind. They came at him too fast for him to fight them all off, and within seconds they had taken over his mind.

"She did what she has to!" He covered his eyes with his hands and answered the doctor. "She has no choice. Her pain…you can't conceive of her pain. She's showed us only the tiniest fraction of it, and look at what it has done…Andrew…"

As hard as he tried, Margold couldn't fight his tears. The wall was gone, and he felt every emotion he had hidden from come back and reclaim his psyche.

"Where did she visit you? Where can I find her?" the doctor asked.

Margold removed his hands from his eyes, and he stood up and grabbed the doctor by his arms.

"Don't look for her!" he shouted. "She has no choice! She'll show it to you too! You'll feel it and you'll end up just like us! JUST LIKE US!"

An orderly heard Margold's shouting and ran into his room and pushed him away from the startled doctor. Margold fought against him and continued to shout.

"We've only been given a glimpse! Imagine what she sees! What she feels! She can't help it! She has no choice!"

A nurse ran in with a syringe and gave Margold a shot. Within seconds his words began to slur and his eyelids grew heavy. He began to shake and tears continued to fall from his eyes.

"She has no choice..." he whispered quietly before he faded into unconsciousness.

• • •

Three months passed before Melanie decided she was strong enough. Everyone she knew told her it was too soon and that her plan was insane no matter how fit she was, but she was resolved. She found new positions in other households for all her servants and then sold every possession she could, including their home. Legally she had no right to do so while Andrew was still alive, but the sums she accepted were so low no one brought this up.

With the money she had earned, she bought and bribed her way throughout the country. She traveled through an underground set up by Confederate supporters living in Union states, which meant she had to hide in cellars during the day and move swiftly at night. Twice she was confronted by Union soldiers who had questioned why she was out so late at night, and both times she managed to use her femininity to convince them that her motives were purely innocent. Had she been a man, she would not have been so fortunate.

It had taken her three months to get to the bank of the river that she had to cross to get to Andrew. As she shivered in the rain, she took inventory of her possessions, which she had purchased with the last of her money. She had a small rowboat, a pickax, a shovel, a pistol and the dark suit that she wore to disguise herself as a man. These things were all she had to free her husband from his imprisonment. She prayed it would be enough. Finally the rain relented enough to allow her to cross, and she rowed as quickly as she could towards the island. She was tired and sore, but she pushed herself harder than she ever had before, ignoring the pain that tortured her arms and legs. Because of the rain the water was so high, and her boat hit land just 20 feet from the stone wall of the base. Her dark suit helped to hide her in the night air as she tied the boat up and searched for an opening into the base.

Before she had left home, she had once again spoken to the young soldier who had first told her of Andrew's imprisonment. From him she learned about the base's weaknesses and where her best chances for entry could be found. Over six months had elapsed since the young man had been at the prison, so there was a good chance that his information would prove to be out of date. Melanie knew what would happen to her if she were caught, but even then it would be worth it if she got to see Andrew at least once before she was executed.

What she did not know was that the rain she had cursed so vehemently would turn out to be key in helping her get

inside the base. Already undermanned, the handful of Union soldiers who guarded the base's walls at night had been called inside to help deal with the flooding that was carrying off and damaging important supplies. As they piled sandbags and bailed water, Melanie was able to sneak inside without anyone noticing.

Once she was inside, her heart began to race with a combination of fear and elation. She was as close as she could ever hope to be, but she still risked being caught and faced the horrible possibility that something had happened to Andrew during the past several months. She heard the sound of men shouting to her right, so she went left, trying her best to remember the directions she had gotten from the young soldier. The rain, having lessened for the time she had rowed across the water, started to fall more heavily. The water rose from the ground and, as she inched forward, eventually reached her shins. She had to stop several times when she heard the sounds of approaching Union soldiers, but each time she had managed to go undetected. Finally, after two hours of agonizingly slow progress she reached the area of the base where the prisoners were held. There she saw that just one man guarded it, though the young soldier had warned her to expect at least the three. The other two guards were on flood duty, which meant that getting to Andrew would be easier then she had anticipated.

Bored and uncomfortable in the rain, the man standing guard didn't notice as she crept behind him, holding the shovel she had carried with her. Swinging it as hard as she could, she slammed it into the back of the man's head. He grunted painfully and fell face-first into the water. She turned him over and searched him for the key to the door behind them. She had to stifle her desire to shout out with joy when she found it and used it to open the door.

She saw heads pop up from the cells as she walked through the door. All the men looked the same, with long scraggly beards and clothes that had grown ragged and worn. For a moment she was afraid that she might not recognize Andrew, but that fear vanished when she took off the hat she had been wearing and her long auburn hair fell to her shoulders. It was then that she heard a voice shout out to her.

"Melanie!" Andrew cried out. "What are you doing here?"

"I'm making sure you keep your promise," she told him as she ran to his cell and unlocked it with her key. Freed, Andrew grabbed his wife and hugged her as hard as he could. She hugged him back and kissed him deeply on the lips. Knowing the danger of their situation, they quickly ended their celebration and started unlocking the other cells.

There were too many men to escape from where Melanie had come in, which was why she had brought the shovel and pickax. The freed men ran to the back of the prison, which had been built on top of the ground with no attempt at flooring, and began to dig as fast as they could. Like the rest of the base, the prison was flooded with water, which made the digging that much more difficult. Still, there were many smart men working on the problem, and they devised a method that kept the process as dry as possible. It still took a lot longer than they would have liked, and the rain finally stopped falling and the sun started to rise just as they neared completion. Together they decided they had gone too far to stop now, so they continued. Finally, they created a hole large enough to crawl through, and they lined up to pass through it. Andrew and Melanie stood at the back of the line, holding each other's hand. They waited as the others crawled through the muck to the other side and made a break for freedom. They were just about to crawl in themselves when they were stopped by the sound of a fired pistol.

Behind them stood the colonel who had fired the shot. They turned to face him and saw that with him were five armed soldiers who aimed their weapons directly at them. Out of instinct, Andrew lunged forward to protect his wife, but he stopped at her command.

"Andrew, don't!" she ordered him.

"Listen to the woman," the colonel advised him, "bravery will only get you killed." He turned and ordered three of his men to inform the other soldiers that prisoners had escaped. "Be quick," he told them, "they can't have gotten far." The three men left, leaving the other two with their weapons still pointed at Melanie and Andrew.

During this distraction, Melanie slipped her hand into her suit and pulled out the pistol she had brought when she had gotten the tools and the boat. While the colonel looked away she pointed it at him and pulled the trigger.

• • •

The rain finally stopped falling. The electricity went back on, and the generators were shut off. A message on the intercom informed everyone that the roads were now safe to drive on and they could go home, assuming that their shift wasn't about to start.

Eugenia hugged her husband gratefully when he came through their door, and he hugged her back. Then he went to sleep, praying that he would not be woken by another phone call. He wasn't.

Five months passed without incident. Margold went back to staring at his wall, and had thus far avoided the same fate as the others, and the doctor became too distracted by other concerns to worry about the base's unusual problem.

Then one quiet Wednesday night, as he walked to his car with an umbrella to protect him from the light drizzle outside, he caught a glimpse of something unusual out of the corner of his eye. It lasted for just a second before it vanished from his sight. Curious, he walked to where he had spotted it. When he got there, it flashed again in the periphery of his vision. This happened seven more times. Each time the flash occurred just when he got to where he had thought he had seen it, and always to his side, never directly in front of him. About to give up, he turned and realized that he didn't recognize where he was. He was in a part of the base he had never seen before. It was a quiet secluded spot, where no one could see him. Exactly the sort of space a person would lead you to if they wanted to talk to you without anyone interrupting.

Suddenly frightened, the doctor tried to run out from the spot, but he was stopped by the figure that had led him there. This time it appeared directly in front of him, and it did not vanish as soon as he saw it. It was dressed in a long dark robe.

"Hello doctor," it spoke to him as it pulled down the hood that covered its head.

Her hair was long and auburn, her smile was sympathetic and she looked like a fairy queen. Her sadness only made her natural beauty more obvious.

She told him her name.

. . .

She pulled the trigger and expected to see the colonel fall to the ground in front of her, but he did not fall. He did not fall. As hard as she stared, he did not fall.

The pistol was damp. It was old and it was damp. Her aim had been perfect, and the colonel should have fallen, but the pistol was damp. She screamed as it exploded in her hand. She screamed as its fragments flew out past her. She screamed as the bullet meant for the colonel killed Andrew instead.

She screamed as he fell to the ground, and she screamed as the soldiers grabbed her and dragged her away from his body. She screamed until the colonel could take the sound no more and slammed the handle of his pistol into the back of her head. Even then she still screamed, but her cries were heard only inside her own mind.

When she awoke, she found herself in one of the cells. She looked around and saw that many of the men who escaped had been found and returned. She learned that several had been shot and a handful had managed to get away. She also learned that the soldier she had knocked out with her shovel had drowned while he lay on the flooded ground and for that—along with organizing the escape attempt—she was going to be executed. She was going to hang.

She could not bring herself to care. Her life was already over. It had ended when the pistol misfired and killed the one person for whom she had willingly sacrificed everything she had to protect. She was already dead; those around her just didn't know it yet.

She did not weep. She did not cry. Her face was a blank mask of stoic fatalism. She sat in her cell and she waited. She did not speak. She did not eat. She just waited. When she slept, she dreamt about the noose. She dreamt that when the rope tightened and snapped her neck she would see Andrew once again. Then she would awake and wonder why they were taking so long.

What she did not know was that—though the Union soldiers were her enemy—they were not cruel or heartless. They took no pleasure in the idea of seeing her die. Though her crimes were serious and could not be ignored, they understood why she had committed them. Many of them wished that they knew the love of woman so determined and strong. Because they felt some sympathy for her, and with the blessing of the colonel whom she had intended to kill, she was asked if she had a last request.

Melanie now only thought about meeting her husband in the world after this one, and as she looked down at the dark suit she wore, she knew then what to ask for.

"If you could find me a dress," she told the guard who had asked her what she wanted, "I would be most grateful."

At first the Union soldiers were unsure if they could fulfill her last desire, because there were no other women around and the nearest town was too far away, but then the colonel remembered that a traveling theater group had once visited and had accidentally left behind a trunk full of clothes. Among these costumes the only one that resembled a dress was a long black hooded monks robe, which they gave to her, along with a comb and some theatrical makeup that had also been stowed inside the trunk. They also gave her some water and soap to clean herself with.

She rid herself of the mud that covered her body and combed out the tangles in her hair. She used only a small amount of the makeup on her lips and replaced her suit with the robe. The guard who came to take her from her cell was stunned by the transformation that had occurred. He found it impossible to look her in her eyes, and he stared down at the floor as he told her it was time to go.

Without a word she followed him out of her cell. The other prisoners stared at her as she walked past them. Though they wanted to thank her for what she had tried to do for them, they stayed silent. This was not a moment when words were appropriate. She followed the guard out of the prison and saw the gallows ahead of them.

"At last," she thought to herself as she walked up its steps.

Someone said a prayer as the noose went around her neck. She closed her eyes and thought only of Andrew. Then she fell. The rope tightened, she saw a flash of light and she died. The light faded and she found herself standing below her swinging body.

It was over, but Andrew was nowhere to be found. She searched and searched, but she could not find him. She was alone. She was always going to be alone. This was her punishment, and she had no choice but to accept it.

• • •

Her voice was sweet and southern.

"I am," she introduced herself to the doctor, "Melanie Lanier."

Dr. Sadler tried to speak to the spirit, but she put a finger to her lips and his words dried up in his throat.

"Do you know who I am?" she asked him.

Silently, he nodded.

"Do you know what I've done? To the others?"

Again he nodded.

"Do you know why?"

This time he shook his head. He did not know.

"Then I will have to show you."

With this she moved closer to him and gently placed her fingers around his temples.

"This is going to hurt," she warned him before she began.

She closed her eyes and the doctor screamed as her memories flooded into his mind. He felt her fingertips burn into the side of his head, and he was overcome by a painful torrent of sights, sounds, smells and emotions. He saw the bullet tear into Andrew's flesh, heard his body as it hit the ground, smelled the sour stink of burnt gunpowder and felt an anguish unlike any he could have ever conceived of. It lasted for only a few seconds, but when it was over, he understood. He knew why she did what she did. It was the only way to ease the pain. There was so much of it that it had to be shared. Others had to know. It could not be borne alone.

She removed her fingers from his head and caught him as he collapsed into her arms. "I'm sorry," she whispered as he began to cry out from the agony he felt for killing a man who had died before he was born, but whom he now loved more than he had ever loved anything else.

"I am so sorry," she whispered one last time before she faded away and left him to grieve alone on the cold wet ground.

The Goth Girl

THE CLUB WAS COLD. Despite the heat outside and the mass of bodies inside, Johnny felt a chill take hold of him as he sat and watched the others thrash and dance about to the loud discordant music coming from the band on stage. Johnny had never heard them before, but he liked what they had played so far. They were obviously still learning their instruments, but they were passionate and he responded more to that than he did to technical skill. He closed his eyes and tried to let the music drown out his thoughts, but the memories of the last few hours were still too strong to be disposed of so easily.

He had had fights with his parents before, but never like this. He had never seen them so angry. He thought his father was going to hit him at one point. They didn't understand. School for him wasn't like they remembered it being for them. He had seen their high school yearbooks, and it was obvious that they had been part of the mainstream popular crowd. They had been the ones who had picked on guys like him. He could easily envision his father as one of the football players who delighted in pouring a carton of chocolate milk over his head or punching him in the stomach. He could picture his mother as one of the cheerleaders who laughed appreciatively while taking in this display. They had been the abusers, and they could not imagine how they had managed to raise a son who was one of the abused. They didn't know what his days were like. What it felt like to be laughed at, insulted and physically assaulted not just daily, but hourly. High school—for Johnny—was hell. Not figuratively, but literally. He could not imagine a place that was worse.

That was why, now that he was 16, he had decided to drop out. What sane person would choose to remain in hell if given the option to leave? His parents' threats of a sad, hopeless future spent never earning more than the lowest possible wage sounded hollow and meaningless to him. A lifetime of poverty, in his mind, was nothing compared to two more years of despair, insecurity and terror.

They refused to accept this reasoning. They told him that if he expected to continue living in their home, he had to stay in school. Tearfully, he threw some clothes into a backpack and told them never to expect to see him again. He had slammed the front door behind him and that slam still echoed inside his head, a thousand times louder than the club's music.

He had $647 in his bank account. He had saved all of the birthday checks he had gotten from his grandmother over the years and he earned some money working at a record store over the summer. He knew this wouldn't last long, so— after he had gotten himself a cheap motel room—he made a list of the places where he might be able to get a job. After that he found himself at the club, not entirely sure how he had gotten there. He had looked around for people he knew, but the place was filled instead with strangers, which struck him as odd and slightly unsettling.

He had been there awhile, sitting alone at a table, when the chill came across him. He was wearing only a T-shirt, because it was warm outside and a jacket hadn't been necessary. He hugged his arms close to his body, and when that failed, he pulled his arms through his sleeves and hugged them directly against his skin. This made him feel a little warmer, but not by much. The music from the band's last song faded and was replaced by the music from a CD, which was played just loud enough so people could now hear each other talk.

"You look cold," he heard someone say behind him.

With his arms still hidden underneath his T-shirt, he turned his head and looked to see if this comment was supposed to be directed at him. Standing behind him stood a girl about his age. Her skin was pale and her hair was dyed black. She wore it long and straight and allowed it to hang down all the way to the small of her back. She wore a short black dress and long black leather boots that laced all the way up to her knees. Her fingernails were painted black to match her lipstick, and around her neck she wore a long scarf made out of black silk. She was definitely talking to him, but he paused before he answered her. Not because he didn't know what to say, but because she was the most beautiful girl he had ever seen. The darkness of her clothes, hair and makeup only made the shimmering power of her features more obvious, like diamonds laid out on black velvet.

"It's a bit chilly in here," he admitted when he was finally able to speak.

"Yeah, I know," she smiled. "It's weird. You'd figure with all these people and the weather outside it'd be really hot."

"Yeah."

"Is that seat taken?" she asked, pointing to the empty chair beside him.

"No," he answered, thinking that she probably just wanted to take the chair. But, to his surprise, instead of lifting it up and moving it to wherever her friends were, she sat down beside him.

"I'm Gilda," she said with her hand outstretched.

"Johnny," he replied, while he shook it.

"As in 'Rotten'?" she asked, referring to the lead singer of the Sex Pistols.

"Afraid not," he admitted. "Is it Gilda as in 'the Good Witch'?" he asked.

She laughed.

"No, her name was Glinda. My mom named me after a Rita Hayworth character."

"Who?"

"Rita Hayworth. The movie star. Gilda was her most famous role."

Johnny looked at her blankly.

"You have to have heard of her," Gilda insisted.

"Sorry," he apologized with a shrug.

"Well, you're missing out," she told him. "She was very beautiful."

So are you, Johnny wanted to say, but he kept quiet and just nodded silently instead. He felt himself grow warmer, so he pushed his arms back out of his T-shirt.

"What's that?" Gilda asked when she spotted something on his right arm.

The second worst argument he and his parents had ever had occurred just after he had gotten the tattoo she was referring to. He had used fake I.D. to get it.

"It's a Chinese symbol. I don't know what it means. I just got it to annoy my folks."

"Did it work?"

"Oh, yeah."

She grabbed his arm and held it steady so she could examine it.

"It's very pretty," she told him.

"Thanks."

"I have one too," she smiled, "want to see it?"

"Sure."

She turned around and slipped the left side of her dress down her shoulder, revealing a small red rose on her back.

"Do you like it?" she asked him.

"It's very nice," he answered truthfully. "How did your parents react when they saw it?"

"My dad wasn't around, so he never saw it," she answered as she turned back towards him, "and my mom has way too many of them to disapprove."

"Are your parents divorced?" he asked.

"No, you have to be married before you can get divorced," she told him. "I've never met my dad. My mom only ever met him once herself. From what I've heard, it was a really good concert."

Johnny laughed at this.

"Are your parents still together?" she asked him.

"Unfortunately."

"I take it that you don't get along."

"They kicked me out."

"Really? Why?"

"I told them I was going to drop out."

"How come?"

Johnny shrugged.

"Yeah," she agreed, "I know what it's like."

"Really?" he sounded unsure.

"Why does that surprise you?"

He blushed as he tried to answer her.

"You just…don't look like someone people would give a hard time."

She smiled at this and decided to playfully torture him a little.

"Why would you say that?"

"Because..."

"Because why?"

"You're so...y'know."

"Johnny," she leaned in towards him, "do you think I'm pretty?"

His face went from slightly pink to full scarlet.

"Well, yeah," he admitted shyly.

"Thank you."

"It's just the truth."

"It's still nice to hear it once in a while. And whether it's true or not, it doesn't mean I don't know what it's like to be treated cruelly by other people."

"Yeah, I guess so," Johnny said, sounding unconvinced.

"Why is that so hard for you to believe?"

"I just don't understand why anybody would be mean to you."

"Why would they be mean to you and not to me?"

"Because I'm not like them. I'm scrawny. I have bad hair and acne. I'm clumsy."

"Are those the reasons they treat you badly?"

"Sure."

"But you just described eighty percent of the guys who go to your school. They can't all be persecuted."

"I guess not."

"Then why do you think they focus on you so much?"

"Because I seem so different to them."

"Exactly," she nodded. "On the surface I may have a face that could fit comfortably on any cheerleading squad in North

America, but on the inside I'm nothing like those girls and they know it. It's the same with the people who pick on you."

"But why do people act that way?"

"I don't know," she admitted with a shrug. "I want to say that it's because they fear us, but that sounds too…too…egotistical, I guess. I mean why would they fear us?"

Johnny recognized that this question was rhetorical and let her continue.

"Maybe they're just jerks," she suggested. "Or stupid. Or both. The problem is that the only way to really understand why they act like they act is to become one of them and if we could do that we would have done it by now. Or would we? Would you?"

"I don't know. I hope not."

"I don't think we would," she leaned towards him. "You know why?"

"Why?"

"Because, despite all the crap we have to put up with, we like being different. It's like our brains are run by an Apple operating system and we can't understand why everyone else uses Microsoft. I don't know, maybe we're just crazy."

Even though he had known her for just 15 minutes, Gilda had become, in his mind, not just the most beautiful girl he had ever seen, but the coolest as well. Why hadn't he met someone like her before?

The band got back on stage to play their second set.

"I don't really want to shout over these guys," said Gilda as they began to play. "Do you want to go somewhere else?"

Johnny didn't need to be asked twice. He stood up and waited for her to lead the way. She got up and headed towards the exit. The warm air hit them as they walked out the door. A full moon shone high in the firmament. Its glowing luminescence highlighted the flawless constancy of her features and was reflected in her hair, which swayed hypnotically behind her back with each step she took.

She was taller than he was, thanks mostly to the thick soles of her boots, which—despite their length and elegant design—looked better suited for hard outdoor labor than everyday fashion. Walking beside her he felt common and small. Her beauty was so obvious, yet so entirely unique that it made a person feel as though they were the first to ever appreciate it. It occurred to him that he hadn't met anyone like her before because she could not be duplicated. There was only one of her in the entire world.

"Why are you so quiet all of sudden?" she asked him.

"I don't know. Nothing to say I guess. Where are we going?"

"You'll see," she answered enigmatically.

"You're not a vampire, are you?" he asked with a smile. "You're not taking me to some quiet place to drain me dry?"

"Damn!" she snapped her fingers regretfully. "You've figured out my evil plan."

"Hey, I'm no dummy. It doesn't take much to guess that something's up when a girl like you starts talking to a guy like me."

Gilda turned serious at this.

"Why wouldn't I talk to you?"

"I thought we already went over this."

"Why are you so insecure? So I'm cute. Why does that mean I wouldn't want to talk to you?"

"I don't know. It just does. All my life the world has worked like that. Sometimes I think that I'm invisible. I can sit in the same place for four hours and no one even notices I'm there, so how else am I supposed to react when a beautiful girl starts talking to me for no reason."

"Who said I didn't have a reason?"

"So what does that mean? You really are a bloodsucking creature of the night?"

" I just don't get you, Johnny. You're smart, you're funny, but all you do is put yourself down all the time. Have you ever considered that that's the reason people treat you badly?"

"What do you mean?"

"I mean that for a guy who's smart and funny you can start to be a real drag sometimes. How many times do you need to hear people say that you're cool before you get the message?"

"Once more should do it," he answered.

"You're cool, you nimrod."

"Got the message," he nodded with a smile.

They both laughed.

"Seriously, where are we going?" he asked again.

"Seriously, you'll see," she teased him.

As he followed her down the side streets and alleys that they traveled, Johnny began to get a sense of where they were.

"We're close to the motel I'm staying at," he told her.

"Really? Nice place?"

"Kinda skuzzy, but it's cheap. I can stay there for about two or three weeks before I run out of money. That is if I don't spend all my cash on cockroach traps."

"Pretty moon, huh?" she said, looking up as they walked.

"Yeah."

"Did you know that the word 'lunatic' was based on the word 'luna,' meaning the moon? People say that it can drive people crazy and make them do things they normally wouldn't."

"Yeah, I read that in a book once."

"See I told you, you are smart."

"You said I was funny too."

"That I did."

"You never said anything about me being devastatingly handsome, though."

"Well, a person can only tell so many lies in one day," she said, teasingly.

"Gotcha," he grinned. "We're getting really close to my motel."

"Must be close to where we're going."

"Where are we going?"

"If I told you it wouldn't be a surprise."

"Is it supposed to be a surprise?"

"*Duh.*"

"There are good surprises and bad surprises. Which one is this?"

"That depends on you."

"That sounds ominous."

She smiled sweetly.

"It does, doesn't it?" she admitted.

Johnny was indeed surprised when, instead of walking past the motel he was staying at, Gilda headed towards it.

"This is where I am staying," he told her.

"Really? That's weird."

He was even more shocked when she climbed up the stairs to the motel's second floor and walked straight over to his room.

"How did you know?" he asked her.

"Call it woman's intuition," she said with a shrug.

Johnny reached into his pocket but found that it was empty.

"I lost my key," he said as he searched his other pocket.

"You don't need it."

"What do you mean?"

"The door isn't locked."

"How do you know?"

"Open it and find out."

Confused by what was happening, Johnny reached for the doorknob and was stunned when it turned easily in his hands.

"How—" he began to ask.

"Let's go inside," she interrupted him.

He followed her into his room, which was dark and cold. He was about to turn on the light, but she stopped him.

"Wait. You're not ready yet."

"Ready for what?"

"Johnny," her voice was quiet and sad, "sometimes people make bad choices. They become so overcome by the present that they make decisions that forever affect their future—"

Her statement made Johnny angry.

"You sound just like my parents," he interrupted her. "Did they put you up to this? Are you going to tell me that dropping out of school is going to be the worst mistake I ever make? Because if you are, save it! I've made up my mind."

"Johnny," Gilda's tone stayed the same, "turn on the light."

Still angry, he flipped the switch and the room was overcome with illumination, brighter than what seemed possible from a single 100-watt bulb. His eyes were blinded for a second before he could see once again. When his vision returned he was surprised to see a young man lying still and lifeless on his bed.

"What—" he began to ask, but Gilda didn't let him continue.

"I could care less if you drop out of school or not," she told him. "It isn't your career I'm worried about, it's your life."

"I don't understand."

"You've made a stupid choice, Johnny. I'm here to give you a chance to take it back."

Johnny looked down at the boy on his bed and tears began to fall down his face.

"This doesn't have to be the way it turns out," Gilda told him.

"How—"

"The pills are in the bathroom. You took a lot of them, but there's still time."

Johnny stared at himself and slowly he remembered. The tears and the hopelessness. The half-assed search through the want ads. The final decision to just give up. The pills that had tasted bitter and acrid in his mouth as he swallowed them. The peace that he felt as he went to sleep. He remembered it all.

He turned his eyes toward Gilda, whose sadness only helped to emphasize her beauty. For the first time she seemed to him strange and unearthly.

"Who are you?" he asked her.

"I'm just a girl. One who made the same mistake that you did and was too stupid and stubborn to change my mind."

"I don't believe you."

Gilda frowned and slowly pulled away the scarf around her neck. As it slid away, Johnny saw that it had hidden a long scarlet scar.

"This is the gift the rope left me with," she explained to him.

"Why?" his voice broke as he tried to understand.

"It doesn't matter why I did it. All that matters is that I was young and I was stupid and I made the wrong choice. You don't have to." She pointed to the body that lay in his bed. "That doesn't have to be how your story ends. It doesn't! I am a gift. I am here to tell you that you can change this, but you have to do it now. If you don't, then you will die here and you will spend the rest of eternity regretting it. Do you understand?"

Johnny didn't say anything.

"Answer me!" she shouted. "Do you understand?"

"What do I have to do?" his voice was barely above a whisper.

"Pick up the phone and call for an ambulance. If you do it now, they will get here in time and your life will be saved. If you don't, you will die. It's as simple as that."

"Okay," Johnny answered. Swallowing his tears he walked over to the phone and picked it up and dialed 911. As calmly as he could he told the operator what had happened and where to go. With a quiet thank you and good-bye, he hung up.

"You made the right decision," Gilda told him.

"What happens now?"

"You'll find out."

"Will I ever see you again?"

"If you do I'm going to kick your ass."

"With those boots?"

"That's right."

"Then I guess this is good-bye."

"That's right."

"Thank you."

She smiled. "Don't mention it. It's what I do."

With that she slid her scarf back around her neck, walked over to him and gave him a kiss on the cheek. The light around them faded, and Johnny became surrounded by darkness. He felt tired and he fell asleep.

He was awakened by a sudden jolt of lightning that surged throughout his entire body. His eyes opened and were stung by the bright lights over his head. He gasped for air and saw that a group of men and women surrounded him.

"We've got a pulse," one of them spoke, "it's steady."

Johnny closed his eyes and felt his heart beating. It was the greatest feeling in the world. He never wanted it to stop.